Draw Me Closer, Lord

A Woman's Guide
to a Meaningful Prayer Life

MARSHA HUBLER

REGULAR BAPTIST PRESS
1300 North Meacham Road
Schaumburg, Illinois 60173-4806

DEDICATED . . .

to the Lord Jesus Christ, Who taught us to pray.

DRAW ME CLOSER, LORD: A WOMAN'S GUIDE
TO A MEANINGFUL PRAYER LIFE
© 2003 Regular Baptist Press • Schaumburg, Illinois
www.RegularBaptistPress.org • 1-800-727-4440
RBP5266 • ISBN: 978-0-87227-665-9
All rights reserved. Printed in U.S.A.
Third printing—2009

CONTENTS

Preface

REDUCED TO ITS simplest definition, prayer is conversation. It is conversation between a child of God and the Heavenly Father. This is an amazing thought: God desires to have a personal relationship with us! This relationship is possible through the only Mediator between God and man, Jesus Christ.

We tend to think that the heroes of the faith were different from us, but the Bible asserts that they were "subject to like passions as we are" (James 5:17). From Abraham—who conversed with God about the destruction of Sodom (Genesis 18)—to Paul and Silas—who prayed in a Philippian jail (Acts 16:25)—prayer has been an important part of believers' lives.

Down through the ages, God's people have been praying people. It was said of John Knox that his prayers "terrified tyrants." Martin Luther said he had so much to do that he had to spend three hours a day in prayer.

The supreme example of prayer is the Lord Jesus Himself. The Gospels record the prominence of prayer in His life from the start of His ministry (Mark 1:35) all the way to the Cross (Luke 23:46).

Is it your desire to draw closer to the Lord and enjoy a meaningful prayer life? We can learn from the Scriptures how to fulfill that desire. May this study lead each of us to a more disciplined, purposeful, and fulfilling prayer life!

Prayer changes things. It changes people. Will you allow prayer to change you?

1

The Privilege of Prayer

"But if we walk in the light, as he is in the light, we have fellowship one with another, and the blood of Jesus Christ his Son cleanseth us from all sin" (1 John 1:7).

DID YOU KNOW that the presidential fund-raiser was held in a private home just a couple of miles from here? I can't imagine having the president of the United States in my house! I'd have to clean for a year!" exclaimed Cheryl to her friend.

That would be quite a privilege, wouldn't it? To have a famous person visit us is probably something most of us don't even dream about. But have you ever considered that you can have a privilege far greater than that enjoyed by the family who hosted the presidential fund-raiser? You can have an audience with the God of the universe! In fact, God wants you to come to Him! Let's look at what God's Word says about this awesome privilege, the privilege of prayer.

Since the beginning of time, when God made Adam and Eve and placed them in the beautiful Garden of Eden, the Creator has desired to have fellowship, or companionship, with the ones He made from the dust of the earth. The first two humans had the highest privilege ever awarded to mankind: walking and talking with the Lord, Who had created them for that very reason.

But Satan, in the form of a serpent, tempted the first couple, and Adam and Eve sinned. Genesis 3:8 tells us that when the man and woman heard the voice of the Lord God, they hid themselves instead of running into His arms, begging for forgiveness and restoration of fellowship. Because of their sin, they were driven from the Garden and were separated physically from God's holy presence.

Ever since that terrible day, sin's curse has infected mankind like a terminal disease, bringing physical and spiritual death. "Wherefore, as by one man sin entered into the world, and death by sin; and so death passed upon all men, for that all have sinned" (Romans 5:12). Every human being except Jesus Christ, the perfect Son of God, has been born in sin, automatically separated from the Father. "Behold, I was shapen in iniquity; and in sin did my mother conceive me" (Psalm 51:5). Sin is the great separator. It not only has alienated us from God on this earth, but it also has set us on the path of self-destruction toward an eternity in Hell separated from Him.

1. Read Genesis 3:8–10. How did Adam and Eve feel about their relationship with the Lord after they willfully sinned?

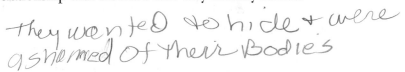

They wanted to hide + were ashamed of their Bodies

But there is good news. Even before He laid the foundation of the universe, God, in His infinite wisdom and foreknowledge, knew that people would sin. Therefore, He planned for people to be able to fellowship again with Him by allowing them to repent of sin and trust in a Savior Who would come to conquer sin and death.

Genesis 3:15 is God's first promise of a Redeemer. Eve's "seed" would "bruise" the head of the serpent, or defeat Satan and all of his evil forces. God's own Son, Jesus Christ, became our Mediator, the only way for us to approach the throne of God.

2. Read Genesis 3:21–24. The first blood sacrifice of an animal

by God Himself covered Adam and Eve's nakedness. Describe their new relationship with God.

Ever since Adam and Eve sinned, we humans have struggled with a rebellious nature and the emptiness that goes with it. We have tried to satisfy ourselves with material possessions, fame, or human relationships, which are often shallow and crumble at the slightest offense. The emptiness can be filled only by the love of a personal and caring God. And the longing for peace is satisfied only when people yield to God and seek to know Him through His Word and prayer. But fellowship with God is often the farthest thing from their minds.

V022

3. What does 1 Corinthians 2:14 tell us about the "natural" (unsaved) person's opinion of the things of God?

he doesn't accept things that come from the spirit of God Because they are foolish To him + he cannot understand them because they are discerned,

4. Read 1 John 2:1 and 2. Look up the meaning of "advocate" and "propitiation," and explain these verses in your own words.

Because of Christ's willingness to offer Himself as the only perfect sacrifice for our sin and become our "lawyer," our fellowship with God can be restored when we receive Christ as our Savior (John 1:12). Not only are we born into His family, but we also are given eternal life. The sin that separated us from a holy God is washed away, cleansed by the blood of His Son. His righteousness covers our own "filthy rags" of good works.

Do you desire intimate fellowship with a loving God? If you have never received Jesus Christ as your Savior, you do not have the privilege of approaching God's throne through prayer as one of His children. You have no advocate. But today you can ask Him to save you, and you can become part of the family of God. You might want to pray something like this: "Dear God, I know I am a sinner. I realize I need Your forgiveness. I believe Your only Son, Jesus Christ, died in my place on the cross for my sins. I receive Christ as my Savior. Thank You for hearing my prayer."

If you have asked the Lord to save you, record the date and tell someone about the life-changing decision you have made. Welcome to God's family! Eternal life, peace, and access to God's throne are now yours.

5. Read Hebrews 10:17–19 and 1 John 1:7. Summarize these verses in your own words.

What happens when we sin after we become God's children? We do not lose our position in His family, but we break our fellowship with our Father. Like Adam and Eve, we may choose to run and hide from God. But the Heavenly Father loves us and gives us the opportunity to restore our relationship with Him.

6. Read 1 John 1:9. (a) According to this verse, what do we need to do when we sin?

(b) What does the verse promise that God will do?

7. Summarize the promises in the following verses.
   (a) 2 Chronicles 7:14

(b) Psalm 3:4

(c) Jeremiah 31:3

8. What does Job 23:12 say about the importance of fellowship with our Heavenly Father through His Word?

As we daily fellowship with the Father, He gives us strength and guidance. If the God Who rules the universe loves us so much and is concerned about our most trivial needs, shouldn't we make it our goal to spend time with Him each day?

9. How does the Bible present God's concern for us and our needs? Read Luke 12:6 and 7.

"But I don't have time to pray," you might say; or, "I'm involved in ministry." Maybe you have complained, "I'm a mother with three small children. I don't even have time to eat!" God knows all about our schedules, and He cares. If your heart is willing and you endeavor to make the time, God will honor your effort. Your decision will not be without its struggles; but its rewards will have temporal (here and now) and eternal results. In moments of fellowship with God, we find that our hearts are cleansed, that He gives direction through His Word, and that we have peace in the midst of the storms of life.

10. Read each of the following verses and note some reasons why we should pray.

(a) Luke 6:12

(b) Luke 18:1

(c) James 5:13–15

(d) Psalm 39:4, 7

(e) Psalm 65:2

11. List some things that may keep you from your daily prayer time.

12. How can you rearrange your schedule to reserve a special time for prayer?

13. What happens when we try to go through the day without God's help and guidance?

Prayer is a gift from God for our benefit. As we cast our burdens on the Lord, He gives us strength to mount up as eagles, to spiritually "soar" above our troubles, and to gain victory over them.

14. What does Isaiah 40:31 tell us?

Prayer is a twofold process. It involves listening to our Father as well as pouring out our hearts to Him. He is able to minister to us during these quiet moments.

15. How does God minister to our quieted spirits?
     (a) Psalm 46:10

     (b) Isaiah 57:15

16. How does God respond when we pour out our hearts to Him?
    (a) Psalm 34:15, 17, 18

    (b) Psalm 55:22

    Victorious Christians know that time alone with God becomes a source of power from the throne of grace. And they know the truth of James 5:16: "The effectual fervent prayer of a righteous man availeth much." The time that we have with our Creator gives strength for today and hope for tomorrow. Prayer is the key to spiritual success. Prayer is the privilege we have as God's children.

> The privilege of prayer every morning
> 'Tis sweet as the fragrance of rain,
> When I bring all my burdens to the Father,
> I know that He is always the same.
>
> My heart—in such anguish—He touches
> And heals all the pain in my soul;
> He whispers, "Fret not, I still love you";
> His words gently render me whole.
>
> I reach out to Heaven for answers
> To questions that trouble me so;
> The still, small voice from the Spirit
> Gives peace, and contentment doth flow.

Our friendship is bonded in worship;
I treasure the moments we share
When I open my heart to God's presence
And cherish the privilege of prayer.

—Marsha Hubler

Put the TRUTH into PRACTICE

1. Do you know for sure that you are God's child? How do you know?

2. Designate a special time and place to meet with the Lord on a daily basis—even if you have only a few minutes.

3. If you already have a defined prayer time, try to increase the length of time.

4. If you have difficulty scheduling a regular prayer time, ask God to give you wisdom in how you use your time. Also ask your family members for their help and cooperation.

2

The Importance of Prayer

"Thou wilt keep him in perfect peace, whose mind is stayed on thee: because he trusteth in thee" (Isaiah 26:3).

I F SOMEONE WERE to ask you, "Is prayer an important part of your life?" how would you answer? Have you come to the place in your Christian life where you believe that prayer is one of the most vital factors in your relationship with God? Prayerlessness causes Christians to live in defeat and to succumb to doubts and fears. But it doesn't have to be that way.

Jesus said, "And whatsoever ye shall ask in my name, that will I do" (John 14:13).

> That is the divine declaration, and it opens up to every praying child a vista of infinite resource and possibility. . . . Without prayer the Christian life, robbed of its sweetness and its beauty, becomes cold and formal and dead; but rooted in the secret place where God meets and talks with his own, it grows into such a testimony of divine power that all men will feel its influence and be touched by the warmth of its love. . . . That, surely, is the purpose of all real prayer and the end of all true service.[1]

Prayer is not only our power source from the Father and the way we fellowship with Him, but it also has far-reaching influence and is worldwide in its effects. We cannot do God's work effectively without prayer. "Prayer reaches up to heaven, and brings heaven down to earth. . . . There is an inner calm which comes to him who prays, and an outer calm as well." [2]

Let's look at what the Bible says about the importance of prayer. We will discover many reasons for developing a consistent, daily quiet time with our Heavenly Father. We will also discover that sin in our lives hinders effective praying. Nonetheless, prayer, qualified by a submissive spirit and confessed sin, should be the foundation of all we do for the Lord.

Reasons to Pray

Write in your own words the reason for prayer that is given in each verse or group of verses.

1. Psalm 34:6; Luke 18:13. Reason 1:

2. 1 Samuel 12:23; Romans 12:12; Colossians 4:2; 1 Thessalonians 5:17. Reason 2:

3. Luke 22:31, 32; 1 Peter 4:7; 5:8. (Look up "adversary" in the dictionary and write its definition.) Reason 3:

4. James 5:16. Reason 4:

5. Jude 20. Reason 5:

6. Matthew 9:38; Acts 13:2, 3. Reason 6:

7. James 5:16, 17. Reason 7:

8. Revelation 4:11; 5:8. Reason 8:

9. Matthew 21:22; Acts 12:5–7; James 5:17, 18. Reason 9:

10. Matthew 7:7–11. Reason 10:

11. James 1:5. Reason 11:

12. Philippians 4:5–7. Reason 12:

13. Matthew 26:41. Reason 13:

14. Psalm 85:6. Reason 14:

Hindrances to Prayer

Sin hinders our relationship with the Lord. "If I regard iniquity in my heart, the Lord will not hear me" (Psalm 66:18). It is possible for Christians to harbor pet sins and not consider a daily relationship with the Heavenly Father important enough to make things right with God or with the people around them.

15. Let's examine some specific hindrances to prayer. Look up each verse or set of verses and define the type of hindrance mentioned in each one.

(a) Proverbs 1:24, 25; 28:9

(b) 1 John 3:17

(c) Malachi 3:8–10

(d) Matthew 5:23, 24; 6:14

(e) Matthew 6:5

(f) James 1:5, 6

(g) James 4:3

(h) 1 Peter 3:7

Matters for Prayer

Since human nature tends to be self-centered, sometimes our prayers are consumed with me, myself, and I. However, as we mature in our faith and our relationship with the Lord, we will want to pray about the things that matter to God.

16. Before you look at things for which Scripture teaches us to pray, describe what your prayer list looks like at this time.

17. Look up the following verses, and list the things for which God has told us to pray.

(a) Genesis 24:12; Matthew 14:30

(b) Psalm 122:6; Isaiah 62:6, 7

(c) Matthew 5:44; Acts 7:59, 60

(d) Romans 1:9; James 5:16

(e) Ephesians 6:18–20; Colossians 4:2–4

(f) 1 Timothy 2:1–3

(g) James 5:14, 15

Prayer is not an option for the Christian; it is a vital part of the Christian life.

> When we pray, we are saying by our action of praying
> that we are dependent on God, that we need His help.
> . . . Prayer is power—power to change us and then,
> power to effect change through us. . . . The good news
> is that when we seek Him in Jesus Christ, we'll find
> Him and we'll experience the fullness of life that only
> He can give.[3]

> I got up early one morning
> And rushed right into the day;
> I had so much to accomplish
> That I didn't have time to pray.
> Problems just tumbled about me
> And heavier came each task;
> "Why doesn't God help me?" I wondered.
> He said, "But you didn't ask."
> I wanted to see the beauty,
> But the day toiled on, gray and bleak;

I wondered why God didn't show me.
He said, "But you didn't seek."
I tried to come into God's presence;
I used all my keys at the lock.
God gently and lovingly chided,
"My child, you didn't knock."
I woke up early this morning
And paused before entering the day.
I had so much to accomplish
That I had to take time to pray.[4]

Put the TRUTH into PRACTICE

1. Review the reasons to pray. Which ones mean the most to you? Why?

2. Review the hindrances to prayer. Which ones cause you the most difficulty? Ask God to help you gain victory over these obstacles.

3. Make a prayer list you can use every time you pray. Does your list include things God wants us to pray for?

Notes

1. E. M. Bounds, *Purpose in Prayer* (Grand Rapids: Baker Book House, 1991), 111.

2. E. M. Bounds, *The Essentials of Prayer* (Grand Rapids: Baker Book House, 1990, 1991), 97.

3. Norman Nelson, *Morning Glory* (July–August 1999), 34.

4. Author unknown.

3

Our Example in Prayer

"And when he had sent the multitudes away, he went up into a mountain apart to pray: and when the evening was come, he was there alone" (Matthew 14:23).

ONE OF THE MOST common excuses for failing to maintain a consistent prayer life is busyness. We tend to think that people in the twenty-first century have a corner on busyness that no other generation faced. However, as we look at the life of Christ, we realize that His days were filled with the "busyness" of ministry. People thronged around Him; multitudes of physical needs were presented to Him; He had twelve men to disciple to carry on His work after He left.

Because of the demands of His ministry, Jesus Christ made fellowship with His Heavenly Father a priority in His life. Often He went apart from the multitudes to pray all night long, to be alone with God the Father, and to gain strength for the tasks that another day would bring.

In this lesson we will look at what Jesus taught about prayer as well as the times He prayed. We will also briefly consider some other Biblical characters who are examples to us in the area of prayer. It is my prayer that this lesson will challenge us to give prayer a preeminent place in our daily lives.

Jesus' Teaching on Prayer

1. Read the following verses and summarize in your own words what Jesus taught about prayer.

(a) Matthew 5:44

(b) Matthew 6:5–13

(c) Matthew 9:38

(d) Matthew 21:22

(e) Mark 14:38

(f) Luke 11:9, 10

(g) Luke 18:1

(h) John 14:13–15

Times Jesus Prayed

2. Jesus prayed at the start of His earthly ministry. Read Luke 3:21 and 22; describe the scene.

3. Jesus prayed before He performed miracles. Read John 11:41–44. What did Jesus pray, and what miracle did He perform?

4. Jesus prayed about the physical and spiritual needs of others. Read each passage and indicate the person or persons for whom Jesus prayed.

(a) Matthew 19:13–15

(b) Luke 22:31, 32

(c) John 14:16

5. Jesus prayed before eating. Note the event in each of the following passages.

(a) Matthew 15:36

(b) John 6:11, 23

(c) Mark 14:22, 23

6. Jesus prayed at different times of the day and for a variety of reasons. Read each passage and state the time of day, if given, and the incident for which Jesus may have been praying.
    (a) Mark 1:35–45

(b) Luke 6:12, 13

(c) Luke 10:1, 21

(d) Matthew 14:19–25

(e) Matthew 26:36, 38, 42

The significance of Jesus' prayer life is so profound that John recorded one of Jesus' intercessory prayers in its entirety. How rich the Word of God is! Right in our hands we have one of Jesus' private moments with His Heavenly Father on the night He was betrayed.

7. Read John 17. To what specific event do verses 1–5 refer?

8. For what group of people did Jesus specifically pray in verses 6–19?

9. Jesus did not pray for the families of His followers or for their wealth or health. He knew the trials and tribulations that lay before them. Therefore, what characteristic did He pray for them to develop (v. 13)?

10. Jesus mentioned "thy word" and "the truth" (vv. 14–19). From whom or from what would God's Word keep the disciples?

John 17:20–26 records Jesus' prayer for His followers who would not even be born until long after the Resurrection. Just think of that! Jesus prayed for *us* before His crucifixion!

11. List the specific requests Jesus made on our behalf.
(a) verses 21, 22

(b) verse 23

(c) verse 24

(d) verses 25, 26

As the Son of God hung on the cross and died for the sins of the whole world, His thoughts centered on others, even those who had despised Him and had condemned Him to death. Some of His last words were prayers.

12. Read Luke 23:34. What did Jesus pray concerning those who crucified Him?

13. Read Luke 23:46. What was Jesus' last prayer?

14. Jesus is now in Heaven with God the Father. What is Jesus doing? Read Hebrews 7:25.

Other Examples

The Bible contains many examples of men and women who prayed and received God's answers. Read each of the following passages. Note who prayed, what the request was, and how God answered.

15. Genesis 32:9–12; Genesis 33:1–4

16. Numbers 11:1, 2

17. 1 Samuel 1:5, 10, 19, 20

18. 1 Kings 17:20–22

19. Jonah 2:1, 10

20. Luke 18:10–14

21. Acts 9:36, 37, 40

22. Acts 16:19, 23, 25, 40

Have faith in God, for He who reigns on high
Hath borne thy grief, and hears the suppliant's sigh;
Still to His arms, thine only refuge, fly,
Have faith in God!

Fear not to call on Him, O soul distressed!
Thy sorrow's whisper woos thee to His breast;
He who is oftenest there is oftenest blest.
Have faith in God!

Lean not on Egypt's reeds; slake not thy thirst
At earthly cisterns. Seek the Kingdom first.
Though man and Satan fright thee with their worst,
Have faith in God!

Go, tell Him all! The sigh thy bosom heaves
Is heard in heaven. Strength and peace He gives,
Who gave Himself for thee. Our Jesus lives;
Have faith in God![1]

Put the TRUTH into PRACTICE

1. Review the prayer list you made in Lesson 2. Compare your concern for others with Jesus' prayer in John 17.

2. Determine to pray about every situation in your life, whether large or small. Start recording the date of answered prayers on your prayer list.

3. Ask your pastor or church librarian to recommend a biography of a person who was known for an exceptional prayer life. One such example is George Mueller.

Notes
1. A. Shipton, quoted in D. L. Moody, *Prevailing Prayer* (Chicago: Moody Press), 90.

4

"I Can't Find the Time!"

"Evening, and morning, and at noon, will I pray, and cry aloud: and he shall hear my voice" (Psalm 55:17).

HOW OFTEN DO you say words like these: "If only I had the time, I would—"; "I can't, because I don't have the time"; "I never have time to—"? If you listen carefully, you may find that you talk about time frequently throughout the day.

The truth is, we all need to *make* time for things that are essential but not necessarily easy. We each have the same allotment of time in a given week: 168 hours. Christian women who take their walk with Christ seriously will make time for things that benefit them physically, mentally, and, above all, spiritually.

Time for things that promote spiritual growth—e.g., Bible reading, church attendance, witnessing, prayer—does not come automatically. Each of us must struggle to make the time for these important disciplines. The Holy Spirit, Who lives in us, is available to help us with our spiritual needs.

1. Read the following verses and note what the Holy Spirit provides for us.

 (a) Romans 15:13

(b) Ephesians 3:16

(c) Ephesians 6:10

(d) Colossians 1:10, 11

Have you ever asked yourself why it is so hard to make time to pray? Setting aside time in busy schedules to be alone before the Lord is a deliberate sacrificial act that is completely foreign to our strong wills. However, once we realize the great value of this time, we will do what is necessary to make the time. When we commune with God, things change! We change!

> When we acquire the habit of prayer we enter into a new atmosphere. "Do you expect to go to heaven?" asked someone of a devout Scotsman. "Why, man, I live there," was the quaint and unexpected reply. It was a pithy statement of a great truth, for all the way to heaven is heaven begun to the Christian who walks near enough to God to hear the secrets he has to impart.[1]

It is my prayer that this lesson will help us evaluate our use of time and help us determine to set aside time each day for the discipline of prayer.

2. Use the chart on page 34 to keep track of your time for a week. Note the amount of time you spend on various activities in an average day and week.

Now that you know where your time goes, how can you make time for prayer? In the last lesson we saw that prayer was important for the Lord Jesus and other Bible-time people. They had the same amount of time we do. If they could make time for prayer, so can we.

Where Does the Time Go?		
Activity	Average minutes/ hours per day	Average minutes/ hours per week
Usual wake-up time: _____		
Food (shopping, preparation, eating, cleanup)		
Sleeping		
Household duties (cleaning, laundry, etc.)		
Paid or volunteer employment		
Activities for/with children or elderly parents (games, appointments, homework, etc.)		
Leisure/hobbies (include TV viewing)		
Personal exercise		
Phone/computer		
Church activities		
Personal Bible study and prayer		
Bedtime: _____		
Total		

Morning Prayer

He who fritters away the early morning, its opportunity and freshness, in other pursuits than seeking God will make poor headway seeking him the rest of the day. If God is not first in our thoughts and efforts in the morning, he will be in the last place during the remainder of the day.[2]

3. Various psalmists wrote about seeking God in the morning. Read the following passages and describe the psalmist's feeling about seeking the Lord.

    (a) Psalm 5:1–3, 7

    (b) Psalm 30:4, 5

    (c) Psalm 88:13

4. Why is it important to seek God early in the morning? Read Psalm 63:2–5.

5. Do you find it easy or difficult to pray in the morning? What could you do to initiate or improve a morning prayer time?

"But," you may say, "I just can't get up any earlier." Or you may say, "I'm just not a morning person." God can help you overcome these barriers as you trust Him. Multitudes of people have found that the best time to give God the attention He deserves is early in the morning. Consider what some people have said about morning prayer.

• Samuel Rutherford, a seventeenth-century Scottish preacher and writer, rose at three o'clock in the morning to meet God in prayer.

• John Wesley, the eighteenth-century preacher and hymnwriter, said, "From four o'clock to six o'clock every morning I pray."

• Robert Murray McCheyne, a nineteenth-century Scottish evangelist, explained, "A wretched system, and unscriptural it is, not to begin the day seeking God. The morning hours, from six to eight, are the most uninterrupted and should be thus employed."

• Francis Asbury, an eighteenth- and nineteenth-century circuit-riding preacher in the southern United States, said he "proposed to rise at four o'clock as often as I can, and to spend two hours in prayer and meditation."

• Sir Matthew Hale, a seventeenth-century English jurist, admitted, "If I omit praying and reading God's Word in the morning, nothing goes well all day."

• General Havelock, a nineteenth-century British major general, rose at four o'clock if his troops were marching at six o'clock rather than lose the opportunity to commune with God.[3]

6. In the following verses, note the name of the "early riser" and the nature of each one's time with the Lord.

(a) Genesis 19:27

(b) Genesis 28:18

(c) Exodus 24:4

(d) Judges 6:36–38

(e) 1 Samuel 1:19

(f) Mark 1:35

Most of us are probably not as ambitious as these examples (Biblical and otherwise), but if we endeavor to revise our schedules or try to get up earlier, we will find that morning prayer is possible.

7. Look over your time chart again. What could you change in order to have some morning time for prayer?

Noontime Prayer

Some ladies work outside the home; stay-at-home moms are often just as busy, if not more so. The noonday meal can be especially busy if you have little ones. Perhaps the only time you have to quiet your heart at noon is a few seconds at the kitchen table with the children or on a lunch break at the office. Thanking God for His help thus far in the day will uplift your soul and reassure you that the Lord is with you every step of the way.

8. The key verse for this lesson (Psalm 55:17) mentions praying at noon. What does this verse teach should be our attitude toward prayer?

Evening Prayer

As early as the Garden of Eden, God desired to fellowship, or commune, with mankind in the "cool of the day," the evening (Genesis 3:8). The evening affords us time to gather our thoughts after a busy day and to rest in the Lord and His promises. There is no better way to close our eyes in sleep after a busy day than with a prayer of thanks on our lips.

9. In addition to the key verse, other passages mention evening and night prayer. Note who prayed (if a person is mentioned) and the circumstances of the prayer.

(a) 1 Samuel 15:10, 11

(b) Daniel 9:20, 21

(c) Psalm 4:4

(d) Psalm 17:3

(e) Psalm 119:55

(f) Psalm 119:62

(g) Matthew 14:22, 23; Luke 6:12, 13

(h) Acts 16:25

Continual Prayer

"How can anyone possibly pray *all* the time?" you may ask. Prayer is a definite act of the will, but it is also an attitude of the soul. To pray continually is to be continually ready to pray; then prayer becomes a matter of divine opportunity each day and not a forced ritual that we rush through.

10. (a) With what heartfelt attitudes should we approach the throne of God each day? Read Philippians 4:6.

(b) What does the word "supplication" mean?

Sometimes we can sit quietly and shut out the world; other times we can't. But developing a spirit of devotion will put God first in everything we do.

> The spirit of devotion makes the common things of earth sacred, and the little things great. With this spirit of devotion, we go to business on Monday directed by the very same influence, and inspired by the same influences by which we went to church on Sunday. . . . The spirit of devotion removes religion from being a thin veneer, and puts it into the very life and being of our souls.[4]

11. Record what each of the following passages says about the time for prayer and our attitude in prayer.

(a) Psalm 88:1–4

(b) Ephesians 6:18

(c) 1 Thessalonians 3:10

(d) 2 Timothy 1:3

> May God's people everywhere come to a fuller realization and appreciation of the importance and inestimable privilege of prayer, and learn so to pray as to greatly increase the efficiency and usefulness of the church of Jesus Christ among men.[5]

12. Look at your time schedule again. What changes can you make throughout the day or week to allow more time alone with God?

> Life has begun again, Father.
> You have given me another day of grace,
> another day to live:
>   to speak to someone,

to touch someone,
to ask for something,
to take something,
to give something.
Whatever I make of this day,
whatever I become this day
I put into Your hands.[6]

Put the TRUTH into PRACTICE

1. Make a copy of your revised time schedule and mount it on the refrigerator, along with a copy of Psalm 55:17. Use this schedule as a reminder of your new determination to make prayer an important part of your daily and weekly schedule.

2. Choose one or more prayer partners from your Bible study group. Set specific times of the day or week when you will pray together, even though you are not necessarily together physically.

Notes

1. Bounds, *Purpose in Prayer,* 32.

2. E. M. Bounds, *Power through Prayer* (Grand Rapids: Baker Book House, 1991), 45.

3. Examples cited in Dennis Corle, *The Discipline of Prayer* (Claysburg, PA: Revival Fires! Publishing, 1995), 7, 11, and Moody, *Prevailing Prayer,* 16.

4. Bounds, *The Essentials of Prayer,* 28.

5. *Daily Meditations for Prayer* (Westchester, IL: Good News Publishers, 1978), 6.

6. Anne Springsteen, quoted in *Prayers for Daily Living* (Milwaukee: Ideals Publishing Co., 1975), 4. Used by permission.

5

Your PART in Prayer

"Speaking to yourselves in psalms and hymns and spiritual songs, singing and making melody in your heart to the Lord; giving thanks always for all things unto God and the Father in the name of our Lord Jesus Christ" (Ephesians 5:19, 20).

J UST SUPPOSE THAT on a vacation in England you asked for—and received!—an audience with Queen Elizabeth II. You would be thrilled beyond compare! In the hours before the appointed visit, you would probably buy new clothes, get your hair done, have a manicure, and quickly learn lessons in court protocol. Nothing would stop you from making sure you would make the best impression possible when you were introduced to the Queen. You would hope that in the brief moments you have with her, she would be genuinely interested in you and perhaps grant a simple request you might make. A few minutes with the British sovereign would be an event you would remember and talk about for the rest of your life.

In the spiritual realm, God has given every Christian an open invitation to have an audience with Him, the God of the universe. We are His children because we have accepted the sacrificial death of His Son on our behalf. We are able at any moment to cry, "Abba,

Father" and come to Him whenever we feel the need (Romans 8:15). We are the children of the King of the universe!

We can come before our Father's presence with the confidence that He has our best interests at heart. Although we should humbly seek His face, we never need to fear that He will reject us. Like no earthly sovereign or parent, our King knows how we feel about everything and is eager to help us gain the victory over any problem we might have.

1. What does the Bible tell us about our Lord's willingness to listen to our requests and answer them? Read Hebrews 4:14 and 15.

2. The Scriptures teach that we should pray humbly, yet boldly. Read the following verses and summarize this humble/bold approach to the throne of God: 2 Chronicles 7:14; 2 Chronicles 34:27; Psalm 10:17; Hebrews 4:16.

3. How can we achieve both of these attitudes at the same time? Read Hebrews 10:17 and 19–23; James 4:10; and 1 Peter 5:5 and 6.

The Bible tells us that approaching the throne of God is a privilege; it should not be taken lightly. Let's consider the "how-tos" of coming to God's throne.

Doing Our PART

In his book *Prevailing Prayer,* nineteenth-century evangelist D. L. Moody described nine elements that he considered essential to true prayer: adoration, confession, restitution, thanksgiving, forgiveness, unity, faith, petition, and submission.[1] We can categorize those nine elements into the acronym PART—a useful and effective pattern for prayer.

Praise
Admission
Request
Thanksgiving

Praise

4. How did Jesus instruct us to begin our prayers to God? Read Matthew 6:9.

5. Read the following praise verses and jot down a key idea or phrase that you can incorporate in your own praise to God.

(a) Psalm 9:1, 2

(b) Psalm 95:2, 6

(c) Psalm 96:8, 9

(d) Psalm 99:5

(e) Psalm 100:1, 2

(f) Hebrews 13:15

What a marvelous opportunity to speak to the Ruler of the heavens! As we approach God's throne with a humble spirit and praise on our lips, our hearts should overflow with joy at the realization that we are in God's presence.

6. According to the key verses for this lesson, Ephesians 5:19 and 20, what else can we have in our hearts as we come to God in prayer?

A good reason for memorizing praise portions of Scripture—as well as hymns and choruses of praise—is to sing them back to our Heavenly Father as we come to Him in prayer.

7. Have you used hymns, choruses, and Scripture passages in this way? What songs or Scriptures are especially meaningful to you?

Admission

Honesty and a clear conscience are vital to maintaining a healthy relationship and open communication with other people. Deception and dishonesty break relationships and hinder fellowship. The same thing is true in our relationship with God. Confessed sin and a clear conscience lead to an open relationship, but sin breaks that fellowship.

Yes, God is omniscient. Yes, He knows everything we've ever done. But like an earthly parent who strives to teach honesty to the child who insists he didn't take the forbidden cookie, God desires that we have a repentant heart about those things that displease Him and break our fellowship with a holy God. He wants us to be open and honest about who we really are.

The easiest way to admit our guilt is to make a blanket statement, such as "Dear Lord, forgive all my sins." However, God wants us to say the same thing about our sinful action that *He* says; He wants us to call it "sin." Sometimes we think that if we don't murder, steal, or commit adultery, we have nothing to admit, or confess. But the sins of the "old man" that the Bible commands us to put off are things such as bitterness, gossip, and impatience. Look at the "Put Off . . . Put On" list on pages 53 and 54. This list is an eye-opening reminder that we need God's help every day in order to live lives that are pleasing to Him.

8. Summarize what each of the following verses teaches about admitting our sin as we come to God in prayer.

(a) Psalm 32:5

(b) Psalm 34:15–18

(c) Psalm 66:18–20

9. Read 1 John 1:9. What is God's promise to us when we come to Him in confession?

Request

After we confess our sin to God, we are ready to present our requests to our Heavenly Father. Depending on the needs in our lives and the lives of others, this segment of our prayer time could be the most intense and lengthy. God is eager and willing to meet us in our prayers, to commune with us, and to answer.

10. What does the Bible tell us to do with our cares, burdens, and troubles? Summarize the teaching of these verses: Psalm 55:22; 1 Peter 5:7.

Thanksgiving

It is only fitting and proper that we leave the King's court by thanking Him for what He has done for us.

11. What confidence can we have in our God when we bring our petitions to Him? Read 1 John 5:14 and 15.

12. What does the Bible say about our developing a thankful spirit?

(a) Philippians 4:6

(b) 1 Thessalonians 5:18

13. How should we close our prayers? Read Ephesians 5:20.

Regardless of how deep our troubles or sorrows, we need to exercise thankfulness. "Thanksgiving and prayer are inseparably joined together in the Scriptures. Those who truly pray will be thankful, and those who are thankful will express this to God in prayer."[2]

It is our privilege to approach the throne of God and to lay our burdens at His feet. Regular, prevailing prayer is the Christian's life breath.

Unscheduled Prayer

But what about the times of danger, sorrow, or trouble when we need God's help in an emergency or in a desperate situation? We have no time to praise and probably can't kneel. During a crisis when the car is skidding on ice, the doctor has told us we have cancer, or a loved one has died, all we can do is call, "Help!" Does God hear our cries then?

Our Heavenly Father responds as human parents do when a child screams for help after touching the hot stove or when struggling in water that is just over his head. At those desperate moments, the manners and protocol of child rearing are set aside as we rush to the aid of the child who needs us to ease his pain or to save his life. In an even greater way, God rushes to our aid, helping us through the deepest valley. He is always ready to answer.

14. Describe how God responded to the following men when they called on Him in their time of desperation.

(a) Judges 16:28–30

(b) Jonah 2:1, 2

(c) Matthew 14:29–31

(d) Luke 23:42, 43

A Spiritual Struggle

We sometimes forget that prayer is a powerful weapon against Satan and his evil forces. While we struggle every day to make time in our busy schedules to pray, the Devil goes on the offensive, seeking to defeat us in every area in which we strive to live godly lives.

15. What does Ephesians 6:12 tell us about the battle we are in?

Each of us may wear the armor God provides for Christian soldiers who wage spiritual battle: the girdle of truth, the breastplate of righteousness, feet shod with the preparation of the gospel, the shield of faith, and the helmet of salvation. With the armor comes two mighty offensive weapons: the Sword of the Spirit, which is the Word of God, and prayer (Ephesians 6:13–18). Prayer is and always has been the key. It changes things; it changes people; it changes us!

Learning to pray effectively takes more than five minutes. A quiet time sandwiched between the evening meal and the evening news might be a noble attempt to start a new "habit," but doing so because "the pastor said we should" will produce nothing more than a ritual of prayers that go unanswered. Introducing a new discipline into our lives is always difficult at first. However, once the habit is firmly established, genuine, heartfelt desire will follow in time. Then we will unlock the key to spiritual success by praying as God would have us do.

> Speak, lips of mine!
> And tell abroad
> The praises of my God.
> Speak, stammering tongue!
> In gladdest tone,
> Make His high praises known.
>
> Speak, sea and earth!
> Heaven's utmost star,
> Speak from your realms afar!
> Take up the note,
> And send it round
> Creation's farthest bound.
>
> Speak, heaven of heavens!
> Wherein our God
> Has made His bright abode.
> Speak, angels, speak!
> In songs proclaim
> His everlasting name.

Speak, son of dust!
Thy flesh He took
And heaven for thee forsook.
Speak, child of death!
Thy death He died,
Bless thou the Crucified.[3]

Put the TRUTH into PRACTICE

1. Purchase a journal (a small three-ring notebook is ideal) and divide it into four sections: Praise, Admission, Request, Thanksgiving. In the Praise and Thanksgiving sections, list appropriate Bible verses you want to memorize.

2. As you become aware of the needs of other people, start listing those prayer requests in the Request section of your journal.

Notes
1. Moody, *Prevailing Prayer,* 18.
2. Henry M. Morris, ed., *Days of Praise* (Santee, CA: Institute for Creation Research, June–August, 1999), 38.
3. H. Bonar quoted in Moody, *Prevailing Prayer,* 60.

Put Off . . . Put On*

Put Off	Scriptural Insight	Put On
1. Lack of love . . . . 1 John 4:7, 8, 20	John 15:12	Love
2. Judging . . . . Matthew 7:1, 2	John 8:9; 15: 22	Let God search my heart
3. Bitterness . . . . Hebrews 12:15	Ephesians 4:32	Tenderhearted and forgiving
4. Unforgiving spirit . . . . Mark 11:26	Colossians 3:13	Forgiving spirit
5. Selfishness . . . . Philippians 2:21	John 12:24	Self-denial
6. Pride . . . . Proverbs 16:5	James 4:6	Humility
7. Boasting (conceit) . . . 1 Corinthians 4:7	Philippians 2:3	Esteeming others
8. Stubbornness . . . . 1 Samuel 15:23	Romans 6:13	Brokenness
9. Disrespect for authority . . . . . Acts 23:5	Hebrews 13:17	Honor authority
10. Rebellion . . . . 1 Samuel 15:23	Hebrews 13:17	Submission
11. Disobedience . . . . 1 Samuel 12:15	Deuteronomy 11:27	Obedience
12. Impatience . . . . James 1:2–4	Hebrews 10:36	Patience
13. Ungratefulness . . . . Romans 1:21	Ephesians 5:20	Gratefulness
14. Covetousness . . . . Luke 12:15	Hebrews 13:5	Contentment
15. Discontent . . . . Hebrews 13:5	1 Timothy 6:8	Contentment
16. Murmuring/complaining Philippians 2:14	Hebrews 13:15	Praise
17. Irritation to others . . . . . Galatians 5:26	Philippians 2:3, 4	Preferring in love
18. Jealousy . . . . Galatians 5:26	1 Corinthians 13:4	Trust
19. Strife/contention . . . . . Proverbs 13:10	James 3:17	Peace
20. Retaliation(getting even) Proverbs 24:29	Romans12:19, 20	Return good for evil
21. Losing temper . . . . Proverbs 25:28	Proverbs 16:32	Self-control
22. Anger . . . . Proverbs 29:22	Galatians 5:22, 23	Self-control
23. Wrath . . . . James 1:19, 20	Proverbs 15:1	Soft answer
24. Easily irritated . . . . . . 1 Corinthians 13:5	Proverbs 19:11 . . .	Not easily provoked
25. Hatred . . . . Matthew 5:21, 22	1 Corinthians 13:3	Love
26. Murder . . . . Exodus 20:13	Romans 13:10	Love
27. Gossip . . . . 1 Timothy 5:13	Ephesians 4:29	Edifying speech
28. Evil speaking . . . . James 4:11	Proverbs 15:30	Good report
29. Critical spirit . . . . Galatians 5:15	Colossians 3:12	Kindness
30. Lying . . . . Ephesians 4:25	Zechariah 8:16	Speak truth
31. Profanity . . . . Proverbs 4:24	Proverbs 15:4	Pure speech
32. Idle words . . . . Matthew 12:36	Proverbs 21:23	Bridle tongue
33. Wrong motives . . . . 1 Samuel 16:7	1 Corinthians 10:31 . . . Spiritual motives
34. Evil thoughts . . . . Matthew 15:19, 20	Philippians 4:8	Pure thoughts
35. Complacency . . . . Revelation 3:15	Revelation 3:19	Zeal
36. Laziness . . . . Proverbs 20:4	Proverbs 6:6–11	Diligence
37. Slothfulness (not doing best) . . . . Proverbs 18:9	Colossians 3:23	Wholeheartedness
38. Hypocrisy . . . . Job 8:13	1 Thessalonians 2:3	Sincerity
39. Idolatry . . . . Deuteronomy 11:16	Colosians 1:18	Worship God only
40. Left first love . . . . Revelation 2:4	Revelation 2:5	Fervent devotion
41. Lack of rejoicing always Philippians 4:4	1 Thessalonians 5:18	Rejoice

Put Off	Scriptural Insight	Put On
42. Worry/fear. . . . . Matthew 6:25–32	1 Peter 5:7	Trust
43. Unbelief. . . . . Hebrews 3:12	Hebrews 11:1, 6	Faith
44. Unfaithfulness . . . . Proverbs 25:19	Luke 16:10–12	Faithfulness
45. Neglect of Bible study 2 Timothy 3:14–17	Psalm 1:2 . . . . . . Bible study/meditation	
46. Prayerlessness. . . . . Luke 18:1	Matthew 26:41	Praying
47. No burden for the lost Matthew 9:36, 38	Acts 1:8 . . . . Compassion/witnessing	
48. Burying talents . . . . Luke 12:48	1 Corinthians 4:2 . . Developing abilities	
49. Irresponsibility (family/work) Luke 16:12	Luke 16:10 . . . . Responsibility	
50. Procrastination . . . . Proverbs 10:5	Proverbs 27:1	Diligence
51. Irreverence in church . . Ecclesiastes 5:1	Psalm 89:7	Reverence
52. Inhospitable . . . . 1 Peter 4:9	Romans 12:13	Hospitable
53. Cheating . . . . 2 Corinthians 4:2	2 Corinthians 8:21	Honesty
54. Stealing . . . . Proverbs 29:24	Ephesians 4:28 . . . . Working/giving	
55. Lack of moderation . . . . Proverbs 11:1	1 Corinthians 9:25	Temperance
56. Gluttony. . . . . Proverbs 23:21	1 Corinthians 9:27	Discipline
57. Wrong friends . . . . Psalm 1:1	Proverbs 13:20	Godly friends
58. Temporal values . . . . Matthew 6:19–21	2 Corinthians 4:18 . . . . . . Eternal values	
59. Love of money/greed 1 Timothy 6:9, 10	Matthew 6:33 . . . . Love God	
60. Stinginess . . . . 1 John 3:17	Proverbs 11:24, 25	Generosity
61. Moral impurity . . . . 1 Thessalonians 4:7	1 Thessalonians 4:4 . . . . . . Moral purity	
62. Fornication . . . . 1 Corinthians 6:18	1 Thessalonians 4:3	Abstinence
63. Lust . . . . 1 Peter 2:11	Titus 2:12	Pure desires
64. Adultery. . . . . Matthew 5:27, 28	Proverbs 5:14–19 . . . . . . Marital fidelity	
65. Homosexuality . . . . Leviticus 18:22	1 Thessalonians 4:4, 5 . . . . Moral purity	
66. Incest . . . . Leviticus 18:6	1 Corinthians 7:2, 5 . . . . . . Moral purity	
67. Pornography . . . . Psalm 101:3	Philippians 4:8 . . . . Pure thoughts	
68. Immodest dress . . . . Proverbs 7:10	1 Timothy 2:9	Modesty
69. Flirtation . . . . Proverbs 7:21	1 Peter 3:4 . . . . Gentle, quiet spirit	
70. Worldly entertainment. . Proverbs 21:17	Galatians 5:16 . . . . . . Spiritual pursuits	
71. Fleshly music . . . . . Ephesians 4:29, 30	Ephesians 5:19 . . . . Edifying music	
72. Bodily harm . . . . 1 Corinthians 3:16, 17	1 Corinthians 6:19, 20 . . . . . Glorify God in body	
73. Alcoholism . . . . Proverbs 20:1	Proverbs 23:30	Abstinence
74. Following the crowd . . . . Proverbs 1:10	Proverbs 3:7 . . . . God fearing	
75. Witchcraft/astrology/ horoscopes . . . Deuteronomy 18:10, 11	Deuteronomy 6:5 . . . . . . Worship of God	
76. Gambling. . . . . Proverbs 28:20, 22	Luke 16:11 . . . . Good stewardship	
77. Preferential treatment . . . . James 2:1–9	Luke 6:31 . . . . Love neighbor as self	
78. Presumption on the future Proverbs 27:1	James 4:14–16. . . . . Trust God's will	

6

Prayer in the Home

"That the generation to come might know them, even the children which should be born; who should arise and declare them to their children: That they might set their hope in God, and not forget the works of God, but keep his commandments" (Psalm 78:6, 7).

THUS FAR WE HAVE LEARNED that prayer is an important part of any Christian's walk with the Lord. Therefore, praying as a couple and helping our children to develop a love for prayer and to see the need for it in their own lives are two important aspects of our lives as Christians first and as spouses and/ or parents next.

Teaching Children to Pray

Christian mothers long to see their children (regardless of their ages) grow in the nurture and admonition of the Lord. Christian ladies who have no children of their own but who have nieces, nephews, or other significant children in their lives also share that desire. We all want the best that God has to offer for each one of these loved ones.

Let's review what the Scriptures teach about praying with our children and then discover helpful ways to encourage us as we impart these truths to the next generation.

1. According to Deuteronomy 6:6–8 and Ephesians 6:4, how should parents teach their children about the things of God?

It is never too soon to teach children about the things of God, particularly prayer. By the time children reach the age where they understand verbal commands, they can start learning about the one true God Who listens to their prayers. Mothers (or any adults) who teach children bedtime or mealtime prayers are already helping to instill in the children a love for their Lord and a desire to please Him. But much more is involved in teaching the concept of prayer than simply praying at bedtime, mealtimes, or even at church.

2. Because children—especially younger children—learn by imitation, what is the best way to teach them about prayer?

3. Name some situations/times when children may be able to observe adults praying.

We have the benefit of all kinds of Christian aids to help us instill Biblical principles in our children. Besides the Bible and a vast array of written material, such as children's devotionals and devotional hymnbooks, numerous audio and visual aids are available to help us teach children about God and prayer.

4. The following verses contain principles we can use in teaching our children. How can we apply these principles as we seek to teach our children to pray?

(a) Psalm 101:3

(b) Proverbs 23:26

(c) Psalm 44:1

5. Suggest various resources adults can use to teach children to pray.

If we teach children to pray only at mealtimes, bedtime, or in church, they may tend to put God in a box. They may think that He

listens or watches only during those specific times. But our God is a
God Who cares for and loves us all the time. We can use Scripture to
instill this principle in the lives of children and to teach them that
they can pray anytime.

6. How can memorizing the following Scriptures help children
understand the omniscience and omnipresence of our God and His
ability to hear their prayers anytime?

(a) Hebrews 13:5

(b) Psalm 34:6

(c) Proverbs 15:3

Teaching children to pray for those in authority over us is essential in helping our children develop a healthy respect for our government and its workers.

7. What do Romans 13:1 and 1 Timothy 2:1 and 2 teach about
Christians and their relationship with the government?

Praying at different times of the day about different issues—such as a sick relative, an upcoming trip, a lost item, or missionaries—greatly reinforces the idea that God listens all the time.

One mother uses sounds that often incite fear to teach her four children to pray. "Whenever we hear a jet flying overhead or a police or fire siren, we take time to pray for those in authority or those in the military," she explained. "It doesn't matter what we are doing or where we are. We pause and pray right then for those servants of the government, even though we do not know them."

Another mother tapes photos of her church's missionaries to the refrigerator door. At every meal the children choose one missionary for whom to pray. "Before long the children know every missionary family and what country they represent. The missionaries become part of our family through prayer."

Praying for "big" things like missionaries with children can be relatively easy compared to praying about "little" things that trouble children of all ages. Helping children, especially younger ones, to overcome their fears can be a difficult concern for any adult to tackle.

8. How can teaching children to pray help them overcome their fears? Read Philippians 4:13 and Psalm 34:17.

Praying for Our Children

Whenever we pray for our children, we should do it as if we are interceding for their lives. In essence, that is exactly what we are doing. Although we easily remember that God has a perfect plan for our children's lives, we need to remember that Satan has a plan as well. He will use any means necessary to destroy our children, including drugs, alcohol, sex, rebellion, accidents, or disease. However, he will not be able to use any of these devices for his purposes if we defeat him with the strongest spiritual weapon available to us: prayer.

9. As we pray for our children and do all we can to bring them up in the nurture and admonition of the Lord, what must we realize concerning them? Read 1 Samuel 1:27 and 28.

10. We can pray about many things regarding our children; e.g., their safety, their health, friendships, school concerns, their future mates. However, of all the prayers we can utter for our children, which one is most important? Read Romans 10:9.

Praying Scripture back to God is one of the best ways to pray on behalf of our children. The Bible is overflowing with promises to all those who love the Lord. As we read the Bible and develop burdens for our loved ones, we can choose verses that are full of meaning for our families and ourselves.

Let's look at Proverbs 3:5 and 6 and then look at it a second time, personalizing it for a child named Matt. "Trust in the LORD with all thine heart; and lean not unto thine own understanding. In all thy ways acknowledge him, and he shall direct thy paths." To personalize that passage, you could pray something like this: "Dear God, I pray that Matt will trust in You with all his heart. Give him strength to lean not on his own understanding. Lord, help Matt to acknowledge You in all his ways. Please direct his paths."

11. List some verses that you could pray back to God for the children in your life.

It is heartbreaking for any Christian parent to try to rear a child in a godly manner only to see that child stray from Biblical beliefs as he or she matures through the teen years. A parent's prayers should not decrease but rather intensify as the parent reaffirms on a regular basis his or her love for the wayward child.

12. How do these Scriptures encourage parents to continue praying for wayward children?
    (a) 1 Corinthians 13:4–7

    (b) Hebrews 10:23

    (c) 1 Corinthians 15:58

Praying with Your Husband

God sends strength from on High to any Christian home when a husband and wife pray together. Those women who are fortunate enough to have husbands who pray with them have a powerful weapon to defeat Satan, who has the ultimate goal of destroying their families.

13. What kinds of weapons does God provide every day? Read 2 Corinthians 10:4.

14. According to Matthew 18:19, what is God's promise to a praying couple?

Besides praying together at mealtimes and bedtime, a husband and wife can also share in praying for their children in other ways in their home. Some couples go into a child's bedroom and pray for the child. Couples can pray together for their children's future mates, or they can pray over a vehicle that a teen child drives. Some couples band together with other parents in prayer clubs, praying together for their children in weekly or monthly meetings.[1]

15. What part of Joshua 24:15 could a couple pray together?

Regardless of the circumstances, couples can be assured that God hears their prayers, whether they pray for their children, their church, the government, or numerous other issues.

16. What does Jeremiah 33:3 promise?

Praying for Your Husband

Christian wives have the responsibility to pray for their husbands, whether or not their husbands know the Lord. The Bible teaches that ladies assume an important role of encouragement and support in a marriage.

17. Summarize a wife's role as described in Ephesians 5:22–24.

18. List five important areas in which wives can pray for their husbands.

19. What ideas for praying for husbands do the following verses suggest?
      (a) Psalm 133:1

      (b) John 13:34

      (c) James 1:5

Many Christian women have the unfortunate circumstance of living with an unsaved husband. Although the strain on the marital relationship can be great, God can help a Christian wife be the testimony she should be to her husband. Since encouraging a husband to go to church can often be interpreted as nagging, praying diligently for the husband and being a silent witness are the best ways to win a husband to Christ.

From Adam and Eve, the first couple placed on this earth, God has regarded the family as the most important institution for loving one another and training the next generation in the things of the Lord. At our disposal is the spiritual weapon of prayer, which gives strength from God to every man, woman, or child who reaches out and embraces prayer as a vital part of their spiritual lives. Prayer can and will affect the family in a positive way. Pray . . . and allow God to work in your family!

> Ere you left your room this morning
> Did you think to pray?
> In the name of Christ, our Saviour,
> Did you ask for loving favor,
> As a shield today?
>
> Oh, how praying rests the weary!
> Prayer will change the night to day;
> So when life seems dark and dreary,
> Don't forget to pray.
>
> —Mrs. M. A. Kidder

Put the TRUTH into PRACTICE

1. Outline a plan that will encourage the significant children in your life to pray at all times of the day, not just at mealtimes and bedtime. How will you put this plan into action?

2. Visit your Christian bookstore, a Christian Web site, or your church library to find various resources you could use to teach your children to pray.

3. Whether your husband is a believer or not, determine to be faithful in church attendance, Bible reading, and prayer as a testimony of God's faithfulness to you and your faithfulness to Him.

Notes
1. For information on a program called "Moms In Touch," see the following article: Daria Greening, "Moms In Touch: Interceding through Prayer on Behalf of Kids and Teachers," *The Baptist Bulletin* (April 2001), 20–22.

7

Prayer and the Church

"I will therefore that men pray every where, lifting up holy hands, without wrath and doubting" (1 Timothy 2:8).

OUR HEAVENLY FATHER'S PLAN for believers includes a local gathering that we call "the church." God intended the church body to meet regularly for praise, worship, and the strengthening of our faith.

When you enter your church on "prayer meeting night," you probably pick up a list of people and needs to pray for. Your prayer on their behalf is called intercessory prayer. God desires for us to pray for the needs of fellow Christians who worship with us in the local church, as well as for those serving in other ministries in different parts of the world. In this lesson we will discuss the many different aspects of prayer and the church.

Praying for Leadership in the Church

1. List all the positions of leadership in your local church that come to your mind.

2. What do 1 Timothy 2:1 and 2 and Hebrews 13:7 tell us about praying for our leaders?

3. Besides his family's physical needs, what are probably the pastor's primary requests for prayer?
   (a) 2 Thessalonians 3:1, 2

   (b) Hebrews 13:18

Praying for One Another

Hebrews 10:24 and 25 tell us in the church to "provoke" (to stir up) one another to love and good works, not to forsake assembling together, and to "exhort" (to encourage) one another.

4. One of the best ways to encourage each other is to pray faithfully for one another's needs. Without mentioning names, list some of the different needs represented in your church.

As we strive to meet the needs of people around us, we might provide for various physical needs, befriend the lonely and helpless, or give thousands of dollars to relieve the poor. All of these deeds are noble and right, but God gives top priority to the ministry of intercessory prayer.

5. Read Psalm 6:9 and 1 Peter 3:12. Explain what God thinks about our ministry of prayer.

Praying for Missionaries and Other Supported Ministries

Missionaries' needs are great. We can add their needs to our prayer journals, praying faithfully about them every day.

6. What kinds of needs do you think missionaries have?

A pastor in Pennsylvania has devised the following seven-day plan to pray for missionaries.[1]

Sunday: Pray for the missionary's spiritual life (Jeremiah 15:16).
- Consistent and profitable devotions
- Good times in the Word
- Awareness of God's power
- Personal purity

Monday: Pray for the missionary's ministry (Daniel 12:3).
- Open doors for evangelism

- Good use of time
- Boldness
- Training of nationals for leadership

Tuesday: Pray for the missionary's family (Hebrews 12:1, 2).

- A healthy marriage
- Support from the family at home
- Needs of the children (learn their names)
- The example of the family to the nationals

Wednesday: Pray for relationships with fellow workers (Ephesians 5:18–21).

- Ability to submit to one another
- A spirit of cooperation on the team
- Honesty and openness
- Lack of friction

Thursday: Pray for the missionary's place of service (Revelation 7:9, 10).

- Political and economic situation
- Growth of the national church in that region
- Missionary's ability to adapt to the culture
- Visas and continued entrance for all missionaries

Friday: Pray for the missionary's ability to communicate (2 Timothy 4:2).

- Diligence in language study
- National contacts from whom to learn the language
- Cultural sensitivity
- Communication with family and supporters

Saturday: Pray for the missionary's physical and emotional needs (Philippians 4:19).

- Health and safety
- Financial supply
- Housing, schooling, transportation needs
- Deliverance from depression, loneliness, or anxiety

Praying for Revival

In his book *The Power of Prayer,* R. A. Torrey stated: "Revival is a time when God visits His people, and, by the power of His Spirit, imparts new life to them, and through them imparts life to sinners dead in trespasses and sins."[2]

Revival can come to an individual, a church, or a nation. However, it cannot be turned on and off like a light switch by the pastor. It is not something a local church body decides to do. It is a movement of God's Holy Spirit, initiated by God as God's people seek Him.

7. Read 2 Chronicles 7:14; Isaiah 57:15; and Acts 1:14. Summarize the prerequisites for genuine revival.

8. Read Psalm 85:6–9 and list the six blessings God gives with revival.

9. Read Psalm 51:10. What can we say as individuals as we pray for revival?

Revival, or a change in our hearts, should be our utmost desire.

10. After reading Psalms 85:6; 119:126; and 139:23 and 24, summarize the psalmists' words, which should be our heartfelt prayer.

> Something happens when churches pray. When churches pray, they are acknowledging lordship. . . . When churches pray, they are participating in partnership. Something happens when churches pray. When they pray, God directs them to the right leaders, and then those leaders can challenge the church to go forward in the will of God. Are you a praying church member? Are you a praying leader? Are you submitted to the headship, the lordship, of Jesus Christ?[3]

Praying in Sunday Services

In a church setting, the pastor or another church leader often "leads in prayer," praying aloud while everyone else prays silently. If your mind is like mine, you may have a difficult time concentrating during those special moments of prayer. But God considers all of our worship time important, both to us and to Him. He hears our prayers and is eager to answer when we are filled with joy in our hearts, love for the brethren, and unity with other believers.

11. What attitude should we have when we attend the house of worship? Read Psalms 64:10 and 122:1.

12. According to the following verses, what hinders prayer?
     (a) Isaiah 59:1–3

     (b) 1 Corinthians 1:10

> Sin keeps us from God, but so does inattentiveness
> and lack of expectancy. Let's not miss meeting our
> Lord because we're not alert to His presence in our
> common life. Remember: "This is the day that the
> Lord has made." The Creator is here and He is at work
> today in Jesus Christ filling the present with creative
> possibilities through His redeeming love and power.[4]

May each of us strive to be holy before the Lord, listening more attentively to the public prayer, a part of our church service that we might have considered insignificant before.

Praying in the Midweek Prayer Service

The early church (described in the New Testament) placed a high priority on corporate prayer, or everyone praying together. The believers met as often as time allowed and prayed together for the blessing of God. His power fell, and mighty things were done: thousands were saved at one time (Acts 2:41, 47); the dead were raised (Acts 20:7–12); and preachers were loosed from prison by angels and earthquakes (Acts 12:5, 7; 16:25, 26)!

13. Read the following verses, which are a few of the many verses about how important corporate prayer was to the early church. Summarize your findings about prayer in the early church.
     (a) Acts 1:9–14

(b) Acts 2:41, 42

(c) Acts 6:1–4

Prayer has as much power today, when men and
women are themselves on praying ground and meeting
the conditions of prevailing prayer, as it ever has had.
God has not changed; and His ear is just as quick to
hear the voice of real prayer, and His hand is just as
long and strong to save, as it ever was. . . . Prayer is
the key that unlocks all the storehouses of God's infinite grace and power.[5]

> Revive Thy work, O Lord!
> Thy mighty arm make bare;
> Speak with the voice that wakes the dead,
> And make Thy people hear.
>
> Revive Thy work, O Lord!
> Disturb this sleep of death;
> Quicken the smouldering embers now
> By Thine almighty breath.
>
> Revive Thy work, O Lord!
> Create soul-thirst for Thee;
> But hungering for the bread of life,
> Oh, may our spirits be!

Revive Thy work, O Lord!
Exalt Thy precious name;
And, by the Holy Ghost, our love
For Thee and Thine inflame.

Revive! revive!
And give refreshing show'rs;
The glory shall be all Thine own;
The blessing shall be ours.

—Albert Midlane

Put the TRUTH into PRACTICE

1. In your prayer journal, list all your church leaders; determine to pray regularly for them.

2. Copy the "How to Pray for Missionaries" guidelines on pages 67 and 68 into your prayer journal for easy reference.

3. Ask God if you should "pray without ceasing" for revival in your own heart and in your church. Expect great things from God!

Notes

1. Adapted from William Park, "How to Pray for Missionaries" (Geigertown, PA: High Point Baptist Chapel). Used by permission.

2. R. A. Torrey, *The Power of Prayer* (Grand Rapids: Zondervan Publishing Co., 1955), 228. Used by permission of Zondervan.

3. Warren W. Wiersbe, *Something Happens When Churches Pray* (Lincoln, NE: Back to the Bible, 1984), 42.

4. N. C. N., *Morning Glory* (September–October 1999), 60.

5. Torrey, 17.

8

Turning Gossip Sessions into Prayer Meetings

"Let no corrupt communication proceed out of your mouth, but that which is good to the use of edifying, that it may minister grace unto the hearers" (Ephesians 4:29).

THE SECRETARY FROM Slander Community Church just activated the prayer chain for a special need: one of its newest members, Mrs. Joy Christian, is having difficulty in childbirth.

Let's eavesdrop on a phone conversation two other members are having about the latest prayer request.

MRS. KNOW-IT ALL: Good morning . . . How are you today? . . . My prayer chain captain just called me. Did you hear the latest?

MRS. GOTTA KNOW: No. What?!

MRS. KNOW-IT ALL: Why, that Mrs. Christian—you know, the one whose husband is always away on business trips—is having her baby, and it's not an easy one.

MRS. GOTTA KNOW: You don't say! Which hospital is she in?

MRS. KNOW-IT ALL: Well, Mabel just told me that the ambulance rushed her to General Hospital at 5:17 this morning.

MRS. GOTTA KNOW: What kind of trouble is she having?

MRS. KNOW-IT ALL: I can't be certain, but Dolores told me that she's been in labor over fourteen hours already, and . . . nothing.

MRS. GOTTA KNOW: Honestly, you'd think she'd stop having kids. She didn't have trouble with the other eight, did she?

MRS. KNOW-IT ALL: Not a one. But that no-good husband of hers always seems to be out of town when she needs him the most. He ought to grow up!

MRS. GOTTA KNOW: Does she have any relatives close by who could help with the children?

MRS. KNOW-IT ALL: Heavens, no! They're all up in the Yukon! I have no idea who's helping them. Probably a neighbor or two.

MRS. GOTTA KNOW: You'd think they'd have more sense dragging all those kids from city to city with no one around to help. Honestly! They certainly need prayer, don't they?

MRS. KNOW-IT ALL: Yes, they certainly do. Oh, it's almost ten o'clock. I have to call Myrtle before she goes to work. I'll call you as soon as there's an update. Talk to you later.

MRS. GOTTA KNOW: Okay. Keep me posted. I'll be praying. I'll call Bernice and let her know so she can pray too. Bye.

Unless you are like Mary Poppins, "practically perfect in every way," you will have to join the rest of the human population in admitting that the temptation to gossip has caused you trouble more than once.

Churches are filled with human beings with problems. A caring church will be an interested church, eager to know when there is a problem and willing to reach out with immediate help.

But isn't it easy to get caught up in a conversation that turns into gossip without warning? If we don't guard our mouths with extreme care, we can become involved in chat sessions that dishonor God. Often when we hang up the phone or walk away, the Lord will bring to our minds unkind words we wish we had never said. An important truth to remember is that gossip is discussing someone who is part of neither the problem nor the solution to a current situation. The less said the better!

1. Read Jeremiah 17:9 and Matthew 12:34. What is the origin of our inability to control our tongues?

2. Why might a person be prone to gossip?
   (a) Proverbs 16:5

   (b) Proverbs 24:29

   (c) Matthew 7:1, 2

   (d) Mark 11:26

   (e) Galatians 5:26

   (f) Hebrews 12:15

   (g) 1 John 4:7, 8, 20

3. According to 2 Thessalonians 3:11, what does the Bible call people who meddle in the affairs of others?

4. (a) What damage can talebearers cause (Proverbs 16:28)?

(b) How are we to treat them (Romans 16:17)?

5. Read Matthew 12:36 and 37. Is every word we speak important to God? Why or why not?

God considers learning to control our tongues serious business. Sadly, many Christian ladies who are faithful to their church and serve in many capacities have never gained the victory over speaking badly of fellow believers. These same ladies would never murder, nor would they steal as much as a paper napkin from a restaurant. But they think nothing of carelessly discussing others.

6. According to 1 Peter 4:15, with whom does God equate busybodies?

7. Read the following Scriptures and summarize the warnings or advice they give about our tongues.
   (a) Psalm 10:4, 7; Psalm 34:13; 1 Peter 3:10

(b) Psalm 39:1

8. The Lord considers control of our tongues so important that the Holy Spirit led James to pen an entire chapter on the subject. Read James 3 and answer the following questions.

(a) If we are able to control our tongues, what else will we be able to control (vv. 1, 2)?

(b) Verses 3–8 compare the tongue to what six things?

(c) Verses 9–12 discuss hypocrisy in what five different ways?

(d) How does verse 13 describe a wise person?

(e) Verses 14–16 tell us that bitter envying and strife in a heart cause what results?

(f) What are the godly traits in the life of a person who depends on wisdom from above (vv. 17, 18)?

The inquisitive nature of human beings often compels us to know more than necessary. Therefore, we Christian ladies need to guard ourselves and exhibit godly wisdom concerning "news." It is unessential to know all the details before interceding before God's throne on someone's behalf. God honors the mere mention of a person's name or an "unspoken" prayer request to the church as much as any other request.

9. What does Romans 8:26 tell us about our need to know all the details before praying?

Love for others, in particular other Christians, does not mean knowing all their affairs. It is equally important as we acquire information about others that we distinguish between *discernment* and *judgment.*

10. (a) Read the following verses and contrast the Biblical principles concerning discernment and judgment.

Discernment	Judgment
Proverbs 25:2	Proverbs 14:15; 18:13
Galatians 6:1	Matthew 7:1–5

(b) Write what a Spirit-led Christian will or will not do with information about another person.

> Discernment asks questions until all important factors
> are understood . . . in order to discover root causes
> for the present problem. Judgment accepts hearsay at
> face value and forms opinions of motives on a few
> known factors. . . . [It] openly shares conclusions
> with those not related to the solution of the problem.[1]

Clearly the Scriptures teach that as we mature in the faith—developing discernment rather than a judgmental spirit—our capacity to love and our burden for others increase, and we develop a longing to pray unselfishly.

Andrew Murray, a nineteenth-century Scottish minister and author of 240 books, wrote the following.

> When I come to God in prayer, He always looks to
> what the aim is of my petition. If it be merely for my
> comfort or joy I seek His grace, I do not receive. But if
> I can say that it is that He may be glorified in my dis-
> pensing His blessings to others, I shall not ask in vain.
> Or if I ask for others, but want to wait until God has
> made me so rich, that it is no sacrifice or act of faith
> to aid them, I shall not obtain. But if I can say that I
> have already undertaken for my needy friend, that in
> my poverty I have already begun the work of love, be-
> cause I know I had a Friend who would help me, my
> prayer will be heard.[2]

11. What does God command us concerning others?
   (a) John 15:12, 13

   (b) Romans 12:17

   (c) Ephesians 4:32

12. Based on the verses in question 11, what are the characteristics of a true praying friend?

   A true friend is a treasure, someone to value more than rubies or diamonds. That true friend will listen as you pour out your heart. She will pray for you, as well, without sharing private information with those who shouldn't hear.

13. Read Psalm 26:4 and 5; Philippians 1:3–5 and 9; and 2 Thessalonians 1:11 and 12. How will a true friend love others and pray for their needs?

14. List several things you could say when someone comes to you and starts sharing private information that you believe shouldn't be told.

15. Write Ephesians 4:29 and memorize and meditate on it as your commitment to turn gossip sessions into prayer meetings.

Now let's listen in on a phone conversation about a request from the prayer chain at Community Bible Church.

MRS. GOODNESS: Esther, the prayer chain just called me about Mrs. Christian. She's at the hospital, and she's having trouble delivering. Her husband is out of town, so Jill and I are going to the hospital as soon as I finish with this call.

MRS. HOPE: Do you know who has the children?

MRS. GOODNESS: Pastor has them at his house.

MRS. HOPE: Let's pray for the family right now; then I'll go get the children and take them back to their house. I'll call Ruth and make sure she's lined up meals for the rest of the week.

MRS. GOODNESS: Okay, let's pray. Dear Heavenly Father. . . .

> I prayed for you today.
> The burden we've shared
> weighed heavily on my heart.
> I prayed for you today
> and His Spirit whispered, "Peace.
> Her will is Mine,
> and she is in My care."
> God answered my prayer today.
>
> —Marsha Hubler

Put the TRUTH into PRACTICE

1. Ask God to help you cut short any conversations you have about other people. Don't ask questions about things that are none of your business.

2. Determine to pray right then with anyone who comes to you with a prayer request or vital information about others.

3. If you promise to pray for someone, remember the need, and add his or her name to your prayer journal. Carry a memo pad or piece of paper and pen with you to church and jot down prayer requests.

4. Memorize Ephesians 4:29 and quote it when you are tempted to gossip.

Notes

1. Bill Gothard, *Basic Seminar Textbook* (Oak Brook, IL: Institute of Basic Youth Principles, n.d.), 176. Used by permission.

2. Andrew Murray, quoted in *Daily Meditations for Prayer* (Westchester, IL: Good News Publishers, 1978), 14.

9

If God Is Sovereign, Why Pray?

"Thou art worthy, O Lord, to receive glory and honour and power: for thou hast created all things, and for thy pleasure they are and were created" (Revelation 4:11).

I F GOD IS SOVEREIGN and if God and God alone has appointed all things since the beginning of the world, why should we pray?

That question has been asked by all ages of people all over the world since the beginning of prayer. In this lesson we'll consider the interaction of a sovereign God with our prayers.

1. Read the following verses and summarize the truths they teach: Genesis 1:1; Psalm 19:1; John 1:3.

2. Read Isaiah 46:9; 1 Chronicles 29:11–13; and 1 John 5:7. Summarize the truth of these verses.

3. Read these passages, jotting down important information from each one. Then in a sentence or two, summarize what all of these verses teach.

(a) Genesis 2:7, 16, 17

(b) Joshua 24:14, 15

(c) 2 Corinthians 6:2

Summary

4. Read the following verses, noting the truth in each one. Then write a summary statement.

(a) 2 Samuel 7:22

(b) Ecclesiastes 3:14

(c) Isaiah 40:28

(d) Isaiah 55:8, 9

Summary

5. Read the following verses, noting the truth in each one. Then write a summary statement.
    (a) Psalm 90:2

    (b) Psalm 147:5

    (c) 1 Timothy 1:17

Summary

6. What truth do these verses teach: Job 14:10 and Hebrews 9:27?

The amazing fact to realize about all of creation is that God made mankind in His own image. Humans are distinctly different from all other created beings, with minds that can formulate ideas and bodies that enable us to speak words. Our diversity and creativity distinguish us from all else. God made us specifically to be aware of His power and glory and to be able to praise Him because of Who He is.

7. Summarize Genesis 1:26 and 27.

8. What parts of creation display God's glory and hold human beings inexcusable for failing to recognize His power?
    (a) Psalm 19:1

    (b) Romans 1:20

9. Read Genesis 2:7 and Psalm 8:4 and 5. Because we were made in the image of God, are we equal with God?

10. Why did God create mankind? Read Isaiah 43:7; Psalm 138:1 and 2; and Revelation 4:11.

Although the man and woman fell, God had planned before time to make provision for the devastating choice they would make. Because of Christ's atoning work on the cross, every person has been given a wonderful invitation to which he or she must respond. That "invitation . . . is extended all through the ages by God's prophets; an invitation to make a decision is given all through Scripture. It is God who created human beings with minds that can consider the truth of what is being made clear and can understand the alternative results set forth. Life or death are pretty clear alternatives."[1]

11. People have been given a free will to make decisions. Review the following verses and cite choices God gave and to whom He gave them.

     (a) 2 Corinthians 13:5

     (b) 1 Thessalonians 5:21

We have discovered that God is a powerful, mysterious God. His perfect will and His ways are a mystery that we will never figure out, although people have pondered them throughout the millennia of time. The Bible teaches that God's will is always accomplished in His dealings with man.

12. Read and summarize Daniel 4:35.

A heavenly master plan is unfolding, but we can see only in part because of our limitations. We can, however, without much trouble, see God working every day in our individual lives; thus we stand in awe of His limitless power. In his book *Stretching the Soul,* Ronald E. Wilson so aptly states, "As I watch him work in my small world, I realize that he reveals to me only an infinitesimal part of his plan for creation, only what I need to know—and when I need to know it."[2]

13. What do the following verses teach us about God's plan?
   (a) Romans 11:33; 1 Corinthians 2:7

   (b) 1 Corinthians 13:12

As we ponder why we pray, we need to remember that prayer is a discipline for our good and a gesture of our most devoted love to our Heavenly Father. It helps us see ourselves as God sees us, in need of a Savior and Shepherd. "While God's providence (which we don't always recognize as such) may surprise, startle, overwhelm, or confuse us, it should in the long run call us to faith. It should point us to him."[3]

14. As we study the Scriptures and pray, what will we begin to understand about God, His sovereign will, and ourselves?

(a) Malachi 3:6

(b) Romans 8:28

(c) Philippians 3:10

(d) 2 Thessalonians 1:12

(e) Hebrews 2:9

(f) Hebrews 4:13

(g) Hebrews 11:3, 6

15. When we pray as God would have us do, what takes place in our lives?

(a) Ecclesiastes 12:13

(b) Romans 8:29

(c) Romans 12:1, 2

(d) 1 Corinthians 2:16

In *The Life of Prayer,* Edith Schaeffer concludes the matter:
"The fallacy, it seems to me, which is a terrible fallacy, is to fail to
recognize that *there remains a mystery that God has not explained to us,* which He does not need to explain. We are finite; God
is infinite. We are limited; God is unlimited. . . . *We are not meant
to sit down and say, 'It is no use, because if God has already chosen, then my prayer is worthless'"* (italics added).[4]

God is so GREAT that He has created the reality of
choice in prayer to make a difference in history![5]

Sweet hour of prayer, sweet hour of prayer,
That calls me from a world of care
And bids me at my Father's throne
Make all my wants and wishes known!
In seasons of distress and grief
My soul has often found relief,
And oft escaped the tempter's snare
By thy return, sweet hour of prayer.

Sweet hour of prayer, sweet hour of prayer,
Thy wings shall my petition bear
To Him whose truth and faithfulness
Engage the waiting soul to bless;
And since He bids me seek His face,
Believe His Word and trust His grace,
I'll cast on Him my ev'ry care,
And wait for thee, sweet hour of prayer.
                                        —William W. Walford

Put the TRUTH into PRACTICE

1. Make a separate section in your prayer journal titled "Blessings." Every day list one blessing God has given you; continue the practice indefinitely. (These items are not direct answers to prayer, but blessings or gifts from God that we often take for granted, e.g., air to breathe, eyes to see, budding flowers in the spring.)

2. As you pray each day, try to lengthen the "Praise" and "Thanksgiving" parts of your prayer. Be careful not to use the bulk of your prayer time solely for presenting a "Gimme List" to God.

3. Ask God to help you rest in Him and not to worry about matters in which He has complete control.

Notes

1. Edith Schaeffer, *The Life of Prayer* (Wheaton, IL: Good News Publishers, 1992), 212. Used by permission of Crossway Books, a division of Good News Publishers, Wheaton, Illinois 60187. www.crossway.com.

2. Ronald E. Wilson, *Stretching the Soul* (Grand Rapids: Fleming H. Revell, 1995), 155.

3. Ibid., 159.

4. Schaeffer, 217.

5. Ibid., 221.

10

Does God Answer Prayer?

"And this is the confidence that we have in him, that, if we ask any thing according to his will, he heareth us: and if we know that he hear us, whatsoever we ask, we know that we have the petitions that we desired of him" (1 John 5:14, 15).

IN THE LAST NINE lessons we have studied many Scriptures that teach us that prayer is a Christian's means to fellowship with God. Each of us should want to seek the Lord every day, not only to gain strength for the upcoming tasks but also to glean from His wisdom, which will help us to do His perfect will.

However, at times it seems as though God does not answer our most sincere pleas and cries for help. Doubt can overwhelm us as we wonder, "Why doesn't God answer my prayer?" Or, when we feel totally alone: "Does God even hear me?"

Let's look at the Scriptures to discover the truths God wants us to learn about His response to our prayers.

1. What are some reasons God would not hear a Christian's prayers?

    (a) Psalm 66:18

(b) Isaiah 1:15, 16

(c) James 4:3

2. What about the prayers of religious people outside Christianity? of people who claim to be "Christian"? of church members who say they are "born-again believers" but are not? Does God hear the prayers of non-Christians?

(a) Proverbs 15:29

(b) Isaiah 59:1, 2

(c) John 9:31

3. What specific prayer from an unsaved person does God hear?

(a) Acts 10:31 (Hint: Read all of Acts 10.)

(b) Romans 10:13

4. Review the following verses. Identify the characters and summarize how they felt when it seemed that God was not hearing or answering their prayers. Did the person who felt God was not hearing his prayers have unconfessed sin in his life?

Reference/Character	How the Character Felt	Unconfessed Sin?
1 Kings 19:1–4		
Lamentations 3:44, 54, 55		
Jonah 2:5		
2 Corinthians 12:7, 8		

If we have confessed our sins and if our relationship with our Heavenly Father is pure, it still might seem to us that He is not answering our prayers. As we study the Scriptures, we will find that the answer could be in the form of one word: "Wait."

5. Read Isaiah 30:18 and Lamentations 3:25. Summarize these verses in one sentence.

6. What assurance from the Old Testament do we have that God hears the prayers of the "righteous"?

   (a) Deuteronomy 5:27, 28

   (b) Psalm 18:6

   (c) Psalm 34:17

   (d) Psalm 99:6

7. What attributes of God guarantee that He hears our righteous prayers?

   (a) Psalm 121:3

   (b) Psalm 139:7, 17, 18

(c) Jeremiah 31:3

(d) Lamentations 3:21–23

8. The New Testament is filled with promises that we can claim concerning God's answering our prayers. Read the following verses and cite the conditions required in our lives for answered prayer:
    (a) Matthew 6:7, 8

(b) John 16:23

(c) 1 John 3:22

Plainly we can see that God wants every part of us totally dedicated to Him. In *The Essentials of Prayer,* E. M. Bounds asserts:

> No half-hearted, half-brained, half-spirited effort will
> do for this serious, all-important, heavenly business.
> The whole heart, the whole brain, the whole spirit,
> must be in the matter of praying, which is so mightily

[sic] to affect the characters and destinies of men. . . .
As the entire man comes into play in true, earnest ef-
fectual praying, so the entire man, soul, mind and
body, receives the benefits of prayer.[1]

We've all experienced circumstances in which we felt God did
not answer our prayers. His answer of no is one that we never want
to hear, yet God knows it is best for us in His timetable and eternal
plan.

Our understanding of God is the answer to prayer. Get-
ting things from God is His indulgence of us. When He
stops giving us things, He brings us into the place
where we can begin to understand Him. As long as we
get from God everything we ask for, we never get to
know Him; we look at Him as a blessing machine.
Your Father knows what you have need of before you
ask Him. Then why pray? To get to know your Father. It
is not enough to say "God is love." We have to *know*
that He is love. We have to struggle through until we
do see His love and justice. Then our prayer is answered.[2]

9. What assurance does the New Testament give us that God answers prayer?
(a) Matthew 7:7

(b) John 14:13, 14

(c) 1 John 5:15

10. How should we respond to an answer from God that we think is wrong? (See 2 Corinthians 12:9 and 10.)

11. God delights in giving us exactly what we need. What "spiritual things" should we request when we pray?
    (a) Matthew 6:33, 34

    (b) Luke 11:13

    (c) James 1:5

12. Why does God enjoy granting requests that are in His perfect will? Read Romans 8:14–17.

From the onset of time, God has delighted in granting requests to those who pray in His perfect will. The Bible has recorded numerous examples of people who prayed for a specific reason and of God's granting their petitions. Of course, all answers to prayer worked for the good of the person and toward God's perfect plan for each life. (See Romans 8:28.)

13. Let's review a few Old Testament examples of answered prayer. Cite the person and how God answered.

(a) Joshua 10:12–14

(b) 1 Samuel 1:9–17, 20

(c) 1 Kings 3:5, 9, 12

(d) 1 Kings 18:36–38

The New Testament, too, offers many examples of answered prayer. Some requests were made directly to Jesus, Who immediately answered the petitioners' pleas for help. Although their face-to-face conversation with Jesus may not be considered "prayer," we see a pattern of unfailing love by our Savior, Who gave Himself willingly for the needs of others.

   14. Review the verses and cite how the person's request or prayer was answered.

   (a) Matthew 8:2, 3

   (b) Matthew 8:24–26

   (c) Mark 10:46, 47, 51, 52

   (d) John 4:49–53

   (e) Acts 9:36, 37, 40

(f) Acts 12:5, 11

We have a wonderful, miracle-working God Who has answered the prayers of His people throughout time. As He was in the book of Genesis, so He is today, answering those of our prayers that fit into His perfect plan and will.

Perhaps if we could analyze every prayer we have ever uttered, we would be amazed to find that God has answered or will answer some of our prayers simply through our obedience to the Word. For those requests that we think are unanswered, "Let's ask ourselves if there is a practice, habit, relationship, or misconception which may be blocking the flow of the Lord's Spirit in us. But also, let's never move beyond humble confession to attempts at haughty control."[3]

In *The Discipline of Prayer,* Dennis Corle assesses the sincerity of our prayers as such: "God wants me to pray and He wants me to learn to depend on Him but He does not want me to become a welfare case. . . . God wants me to understand that there are certain responsibilities even within the confines of my prayer life, things I pray about, that I do not just pray about and then forget. There are some things that God is going to use me to accomplish and some things He is going to use other people to accomplish. I need prayers with feet—my feet. You need prayers with feet—your feet."[4] Do any of your prayers have feet?

15. Review the following verses and cite how the person's "prayer with feet" was answered.

(a) Judges 6:36–40

(b) Nehemiah 2:4–6

(c) Acts 4:29–31

(d) 2 Timothy 1:3; 2 Corinthians 1:1; 1 Timothy 1:2

We all have burdens that we take to the Lord on a regular basis. Perhaps we have never realized until now that some of our most sincere prayers could be "prayers with feet." Perhaps in His sovereign plan for the universe, God might have already chosen you as the answer, or part of an answer, to your own earnest plea. Like Gideon (Judges 6), we may find that God had already planned to use us as His instrument to accomplish His perfect will.

16. Let's review some "prayers with feet" that many of us might have prayed sometime in our Christian walk. After the request, read the Scriptures that might indicate that God will use us to be the answer, or part of the answer, to our own prayers. Comment as you desire.

Prayers	Passages
"Lord, please save my husband"; "Lord, please draw my back-slidden husband back to You."	• 1 Peter 3:1, 2 • Ephesians 5:22
"Lord, please save my neighbor."	• Exodus 20:16 • Ephesians 4:25 • James 2:8
"Dear Lord, please meet the needs of those poor folk who just joined our church."	• John 13:35 • James 2:15, 16
"Dear God, please send more missionaries to win the lost."	• Matthew 28:19, 20 • John 15:16
"Dear God, please send the funds to our church to help pay our pastor's salary so he can care for his children's needs."	• Malachi 3:10 • Matthew 6:19–21
"Dear God, please convict others to join the choir so there are more than five trying to sing up there on Sunday."	• Psalm 63:3 • Psalm 100:1, 2
"Dear Heavenly Father, please answer my prayer so that I know You are really there!"	• Proverbs 3:5, 6 • Jeremiah 33:3 • 2 Corinthians 5:7

As God's children, we have the privilege of talking to our Heavenly Father whenever we feel the need. Long before the prayer ever escapes from our lips, He has answered. He has provided; He has filled the need; He has accomplished His will. The decision to accept His will for our lives rests with us. We can blossom in His goodness or wallow in our self-pity. The choice is ours.

Although we might not always understand God's answers this side of Heaven, His response to our requests can be any of the following: wait; no; yes; I want you to. . . .

Our Heavenly Father loves us with a love beyond measure. That love translates into doing what's best for each of His own, His children, who look to Him for help.

All of the four answers we might receive from God when we pray are demonstrated in the following scenario of everyday family life with a loving father and his children.

John loves his four children very much. Bradley is six, Lucille is eight, Ronnie is twelve, and Marta is sixteen.

The autumn season is ending, and John has asked everyone to help clean up the yard, preparing it for winter. He knows that after being outside all afternoon, the children will be hungry. Earlier in the day he had brought home a large bucket of chicken, mashed potatoes, corn, and some brownies for dessert, something he knows each one of them will enjoy tremendously. Now he sets the table so that they can sit down and enjoy each other's company and fellowship with him.

While the children are working together in the yard, their hunger plays havoc with them. They discuss how great it would be to have their favorite, fried chicken . . . and brownies for dessert! They all decide to beg their father to drive them to the store to buy what their mouths are watering for.

"Children, it's suppertime!" John yells out the door at five o'clock sharp.

Without hesitation the four hungry children crowd the doorway, pushing their dirty hands against the house and one another.

"Dad," they all clamor, "we're starving. Could you take us to town for something special to eat?"

"Whoa," John says, "take it easy. It's already on the table! And there's enough for everyone. There's plenty of fried chicken for all of you, and lots of brownies for dessert."

"Fried chicken! Brownies!" they all yell. "How did you know that's what we wanted?"

"Oh, I just knew," replies John.

"Dad," Bradley yells as he squeezes into the house first. "You know I love brownies. May I have my dessert first? I'll only eat one. Please?"

"You just wait, Bradley," Father says. "You will eat your chicken first. Then you may have one small brownie. Did you forget that too much chocolate makes you sick?"

Lucille squeezes through the doorway next. "Dad, my belly is growling like a bear. Could I eat every piece of chicken?"

"No, Lucille, two pieces will be plenty for you," her father replies. "You'd never be able to eat all twenty-one pieces. Trust me."

Ronnie rushes through the doorway next and runs to the sink to wash his hands. "Dad, may I have four pieces? I am starving!"

"Yes, four pieces will be fine. I know you didn't have any lunch. You must be very hungry."

Marta rushes inside the house, excited that her father would remember how much she loves chicken. Hurrying toward the table, she notices it is fully set with everything but glasses and the usual gallon of milk.

"Dad," she asks, "what are we going to drink? Did you forget that part of the meal?"

"Honey," John says, "I'd like you to get the glasses and milk for everyone. Would you please?"

"Sure, no problem."

"And because of your willingness to help," John adds, "you may have first choice of any piece of chicken you want.

"Children," he says as they all sit down at the table and get ready to dig in, "the chicken is all yours. The brownies are all yours. I did this for one reason, and for one reason alone. I love you very much."

With God's help, may we all realize that prayer begins and ends with our Heavenly Father.

> What seems to be unanswered prayer is also a part of [God's] instigation and invitation to communion and conversation with Him on a deeper level. He wants us to know Him more profoundly than ever. When we feel our prayers are not answered according to our specifications and timing, that feeling is really a longing for God and not just for what He can give or do for us. Thank God for those times. By them we know we have been called into a much more intimate relationship than we've ever known before![5]

> As the hart
> panteth after the water brooks,
> so panteth
> my soul after thee,
> O God
> (Psalm 42:1).

Put the TRUTH into PRACTICE

1. Share with the group a testimony of how God has answered prayer for you in each of these ways: wait; no; yes; I want you to. . . .

2. Label a page in your journal "God's Answers to My Prayers." Make four sections: Wait; No; Yes; and I Want You to. . . . When God answers, record the date with the specific answer to prayer.

3. Write a prayer, thanking God for His mercy, love, and grace, which mean that even an answer of wait, no, or I want you is a blessing.

Notes

1. Bounds, *The Essentials of Prayer,* 13–17.

2. Oswald Chambers in Lloyd John Ogilvie, *Praying with Power* (Ventura: CA: Regal Books, 1983), 81.

3. Ibid., 88.

4. Corle, 91.

5. Ogilvie, 88.

LEADER'S GUIDE

SUGGESTIONS FOR LEADERS

The effectiveness of a group Bible study usually depends on two things: (1) the leader herself; and (2) the ladies' commitment to prepare beforehand and interact during the study. You cannot totally control the second factor, but you have total control over the first one. These brief suggestions will help you be an effective Bible study leader.

You will want to prepare each lesson a week in advance. During the week, read supplemental material and look for illustrations in the everyday events of your life as well as in the lives of others.

Encourage the ladies in the Bible study to complete each lesson before the meeting itself. This preparation will make the discussion more interesting. You can suggest that ladies answer two or three questions a day as part of their daily Bible reading time rather than trying to do the entire lesson at one sitting.

You may also want to encourage the ladies to memorize the key verse for each lesson. (This is the verse that is printed in italics at the start of each lesson.) If possible, print the verses on 3" x 5" cards to distribute each week. If you cannot do this, suggest that the ladies make their own cards and keep them in a prominent place throughout the week.

The physical setting in which you meet will have some bearing on the study itself. An informal circle of chairs, chairs around a table, someone's living room or family room—these types of settings encourage people to relax and participate. In addition to an informal setting, create an atmosphere in which ladies feel free to participate and be themselves.

During the discussion time, here are a few things to observe.

• Don't do all the talking. This study is not designed to be a lecture.

• Encourage discussion on each question by adding ideas and questions.

• Don't discuss controversial issues that will divide the group. (Differences of opinion are healthy; divisions are not.)

• Don't allow one lady to dominate the discussion. Use statements such as these to draw others into the study: "Let's hear from someone on this side of the room" (the side opposite the dominant talker); "Let's hear from someone who has not shared yet today."

• Stay on the subject. The tendency toward tangents is always possible in a discussion. One of your responsibilities as the leader is to keep the group on track.

• Don't get bogged down on a question that interests only one person.

You may want to use the last fifteen minutes of the scheduled time for prayer. If you have a large group of ladies, divide into smaller groups for prayer. You could call this the "Share and Care Time."

If you have a morning Bible study, encourage the ladies to go out for lunch with someone else from time to time. This is a good way to get acquainted with new ladies. Occasionally you could plan a time when ladies bring their own lunches or salads to share and eat together. These things help promote fellowship and friendship in the group.

The formats that follow are suggestions only. You can plan your own format, use one of these, or adapt one of these to your needs.

2-hour Bible Study
10:00—10:15   Coffee and fellowship time
10:15—10:30   Get-acquainted time
Have two ladies take five minutes each to tell something about themselves and their families.
Also use this time to make announcements and, if appropriate, take an offering for the baby-sitters.
10:30—11:45   Bible study
Leader guides discussion of the questions in the day's lesson.
11:45—12:00   Prayer time

2-hour Bible Study
10:00—10:45   Bible lesson
Leader teaches a lesson on the content of the material. No discussion during this time.
10:45—11:00   Coffee and fellowship
11:00—11:45   Discussion time
Divide into small groups with an appointed leader for each group. Discuss the questions in the day's lesson.
11:45—12:00   Prayer time

1½-hour Bible Study
10:00—10:30   Bible study
Leader guides discussion of half the questions in the day's lesson.
10:30—10:45   Coffee and fellowship
10:45—11:15   Bible study
Leader continues discussion of the questions in the day's lesson.
11:15—11:30   Prayer time

ANSWERS FOR LEADER'S USE

Information inside parentheses ( ) is additional instruction for the group leader.

LESSON 1

1. They were afraid.

2. Their relationship was never the same. Although fellowship with God was restored, that fellowship was always marred by their sin.

3. An unsaved person does not understand the things of God.

4. An "advocate" is a person who pleads the cause of another; a lawyer. "Propitiation" means "the act of appeasing or causing to be favorably inclined." When we sin, Jesus acts us our lawyer and represents us before the Father.

5. Jesus' sacrificial death and His blood cleanse us from sin. We have the privilege of going directly to God through Jesus.

6. (a) Confess our sins. (Leader: Explain the meaning of "confess." To "confess" is to say the same thing about our sin that God says; that is, we need to name the thought, emotion, or action and call it sin, an offense against a holy God.) (b) God will forgive us and cleanse us.

7. (a) When we humble ourselves and repent, God will forgive. (b) When we cry to the Lord, He hears us. (c) God loves us with an everlasting love; He draws us to Himself.

8. It is more important than eating.

9. The very hairs of our heads are numbered. He knows all about us. We are of greater value than the birds, which He also knows.

10. (a) Jesus took time to be alone and pray. He is our example. (b) Jesus instructed us to pray. (c) God commands us to pray and promises to answer. (d) We are frail, and our days are numbered. Our only hope is in God. (e) God hears our prayers.

11. Personal answers. (Leader: Encourage the group to share their answers. They will probably include things like a busy schedule, varying schedules in the home with young children or with teenage children, out-of-town travel.)

12. Personal answers. (Leader: Encourage specific suggestions; e.g., get up before the rest of the family; pray while driving to and from work; pray during children's nap times; decrease amount of television viewing; pray while doing routine household chores; tape prayer requests near the sink.)

13. (Ask one or two ladies to share their answers. You may want to share this quip with the group: "A day not hemmed with prayer usually unravels.")

14. God gives strength to those who rely on Him.

15. (a) God can speak to us when we are quiet. (b) When we humble ourselves before God, He revives our spirits.

16. (a) God hears our cries and delivers us from troubles; He saves those with a contrite spirit. (b) If we cast our burdens on the Lord, He will help us.

LESSON 2

1. Reason 1: God hears the sinner's prayer.

2. Reason 2: We are commanded to pray; prayerlessness is sin.

3. Reason 3: Prayer helps us have victory over Satan. An adversary is an enemy.

4. Reason 4: Prayer restores the backslider.

5. Reason 5: Prayer strengthens Christians.

6. Reason 6: Prayer is related to missions.

7. Reason 7: Prayer accomplishes much.

8. Reason 8: Prayer glorifies God's name.

9. Reason 9: Prayer accomplishes the impossible.

10. Reason 10: Prayer gives us good things.

11. Reason 11: Prayer imparts wisdom.

12. Reason 12: Prayer gives peace to a troubled soul.

13. Reason 13: Prayer keeps us from sin.

14. Reason 15: Prayer can lead to revival.

15. (a) Not heeding God's counsel or obeying His commandments. (b) Lack of love and compassion for other people. (c) Unfaithfulness in tithing and financially supporting God's work. (d) Bitterness or an unforgiving spirit against other people. (e) Hypocrisy and pride. (f) Unbelief and inconsistency. (g) Selfishness. (h) Marital conflict.

16. (Guide the group discussion toward naming specific types of requests; e.g., physical problems; children and school matters; wayward teens; financial needs; salvation of unsaved family and friends; strength for the pastor and his family; boldness and courage for missionaries.)

17. (a) Pray for safety in travel or through danger and for blessing on others and yourself. (b) Pray for the peace of Jerusalem. (c) Pray for your enemies and those who persecute you. (d) Pray for one another. (e) Pray for fellow Christians and, in particular, missionaries, that they would have boldness to preach the Word. (f) Pray for all men and, in particular, the leaders of our nation.

(g) Pray for sick people to be healed; confess sins.

LESSON 3

1. (a) Pray for your enemies. (b) Pray in secret. If you do pray in public, pray earnestly and not hypocritically as the Pharisees did, just to be recognized by men. The Lord's Prayer is a model of how to pray, not a prayer to be recited in vain repetitions. The prayer consists of all the important facets of God-centered prayer: thanksgiving and praise, confession of sin and repentance, request for personal sustenance, prayer for others, and worship. (c) Pray for workers (e.g., missionaries, pastors, teachers) to serve the Lord. (d) God answers prayer when we petition Him with believing hearts. (e) Our flesh is weak. We need strength from our prayer time each day to keep us from sin. (f) If we continue to pray earnestly (ask, seek, and knock), God will answer prayer. Never give up. (g) We should not lose heart or quit praying. (h) When we live obedient lives and pray in Jesus' name, we can be confident of answered prayer. (Leader: From time to time throughout this study, remind the ladies that prayer is not a "formula" we use to get what we want from God. All of the Biblical teaching on prayer must be taken as a whole. As the ladies will learn in their study of lesson 10, sometimes God denies our requests.)

2. Jesus began His public ministry with His baptism. At this event, He prayed. (Leader: You may want to point out the evidence of the Trinity. Jesus was baptized; God the Father spoke from Heaven; and the Holy Spirit appeared as a dove.)

3. He thanked God for hearing Him before He raised Lazarus from the dead.

4. (a) He prayed for little children. (b) Jesus prayed for Peter that his faith would not fail. (c) Jesus prayed that His Father would send the Holy Spirit to minister to His disciples when He left the earth.

5. (a) Before Jesus fed 4,000 people, He thanked God for the food. (b) He prayed before the feeding of the 5,000. (c) He thanked God for the bread and juice when He instituted the Lord's Supper.

6. (a) In the dark hours preceding daylight, Jesus prayed for strength to preach in the synagogues throughout Galilee and to heal the sick. (b) He prayed all night before choosing the disciples. (c) The time of day is not clear; Jesus thanked God that common people were receiving God's truth. (d) Jesus prayed in the evening. He may have thanked God for the miracle (feeding the 5,000) or prayed about the next miracle (walking on the water).

His prayer could have been for strength for the next day and for the multitudes to whom He ministered daily. (e) He prayed at night for God's will concerning the Crucifixion.

7. (You may want to take time in class to have the ladies take turns reading John 17 in its entirety.) The crucifixion of Jesus.

8. The eleven disciples. He did not pray for Judas, the son of perdition (v. 12).

9. He prayed that the disciples would have His joy fulfilled in them.

10. The Word protects Christ's disciples from the world system and the sin and destruction that accompanies it.

11. (a) Jesus prayed for unity of believers with each other and with the Trinity. (b) Jesus prayed for believers to be "perfect," or "mature," and to experience the love the Father offers to all as He loves His Son. (c) Jesus prayed that all believers be with Him in Heaven. (d) Jesus prayed that God's love will be in all believers.

12. He prayed that God would forgive them.

13. He committed His spirit to the Father.

14. Jesus is praying for us. (The word "intercession" means "the act of interceding"; "prayer, petition, or entreaty in favor of another.")

15. Jacob asked God to spare his life at the hands of his brother Esau, who had hated him when Jacob had stolen the birthright. God did deliver Jacob; in fact, Esau greeted him with open arms.

16. Moses prayed that God would spare some of the disobedient Children of Israel in the wilderness. God quenched the fire and spared their lives.

17. Hannah was barren and prayed for a child. God gave her a son, whom she named Samuel.

18. Elijah prayed that the widow's son would live. God brought the child to life again.

19. Jonah prayed from the belly of the fish. God had the fish vomit Jonah onto dry land.

20. The publican prayed for forgiveness and mercy. He received forgiveness from the Lord.

21. Peter prayed for power to raise the dead. God raised Tabitha, using Peter as His instrument.

22. Paul and Silas prayed and sang praises to God. God filled them with joy despite their circumstances and later released them from prison.

LESSON 4

1. (a) He gives hope. (b) He gives strength. (c) He gives power. (d) He gives joy.

2. (Ask the ladies to share any insights they gained as they kept track of their schedules. Did they spend more time on some things than they realized? Did they find times of the day when they actually wasted time? What did they learn from their schedules?)

3. (a) David approached the throne of God in fear and great respect. The verses imply he was eager to seek God's face. (b) David prayed with thanksgiving for God's holiness, thanking God in the morning for answered prayer. (c) The psalmist was in distress, but he knew the Lord would hear him.

4. So that we can praise and bless God for His power, glory, and loving-kindness. To satisfy our souls with God alone.

5. (Ask volunteers to share their thoughts. Discuss plans to initiate or improve morning prayer times.)

6. (a) Abraham arose early in the morning to meet with God. (b) Jacob actually made an altar in the morning at the place where he met the Lord. (c) Moses worshiped God early in the morning. (d) Gideon needed a sign from the Lord; he got it early in the morning. (e) Hannah and Elkanah worshiped the Lord early in the morning. (f) Jesus used the early morning hours to commune with His Heavenly Father.

7. (Discuss various possibilities; e.g., go to bed earlier and rise earlier; move some household duties or shopping to the afternoon; schedule appointments in the afternoon; use a morning break in the workplace to pray.)

8. Total dependence on the Lord all day long.

9. (a) Samuel had a broken heart over Saul's disappointing performance as king when he conquered the Amalekites. Samuel wept and prayed all night. (b) Daniel prayed in the evening to confess sin. (c) We can fellowship with the Lord as we lie in bed. (d) God will visit us as we pray in the night. (God does not make a physical appearance or give us a vision, but the indwelling Holy Spirit can minister to us.) (e) The psalmist prayed during the night, remembering the name of the Lord. (f) When the psalmist couldn't sleep, he thanked God for His blessings. (g) Jesus often prayed in the evening and at night, perhaps in part because He could be away from the crowds who followed Him. (h) Paul and Silas in prison prayed and sang praises to God at midnight. (They were probably too sore and uncomfortable to sleep!)

10. (a) We should pray with humility and thanksgiving and trust. (Trust is the opposite of worry.) (b) A humble prayer request.

11. (a) Day and night. When troubles overwhelm us and we feel as though we could die, we should pour out our hearts to God and ask Him for help. (b) Always. We should be in prayer for others. (c) Night and day. We should petition God on behalf of others. (d) Night and day; without ceasing. We should pray with thanksgiving and with a concern for others.

12. (Encourage the ladies to look for places where they waste time or where good activities may crowd out the better activities. Help ladies understand they can pray while they are doing other things [e.g., washing dishes, driving alone in the car, exercising, folding laundry, waiting for an appointment, vacuuming the house], while their children nap, or when they lie awake at night. Discuss the possibility of going to bed earlier at night to allow for rising earlier in the morning. Review the prayer partner plan [see item 2 on page 42], and encourage the ladies to choose at least one partner if they have not done so yet.)

LESSON 5

1. Jesus, our Advocate and High Priest, experienced all human emotions on earth as a human. He sympathizes with us and wants to help us with all our problems.

2. If we approach God without a proud spirit, God will answer. He will lift us up. "Boldness" refers to confidence that He knows what is best for us.

3. If we submit ourselves to God and come before Him in humility, He will give us the boldness (confidence, not pride) to approach His throne and present our petitions to Him with great expectation.

4. We are to pray to our Heavenly Father with reverence.

5. (Leader: Have ladies share the phrases or ideas they wrote down. Mention that the Scriptures—and particularly the book of Psalms—are filled with praise to God. In the "praise" part of praying, we want to focus on Who God is—His character and His wonderful attributes.)

6. Psalms, hymns, and spiritual songs.

7. Personal answers. (Ask volunteers to share their answers.)

8. (a) When we confess, God forgives. (b) God hears the prayers of those who are righteous; He is against those who do evil. (c) Sin leads to unanswered prayer.

9. He is faithful and just to forgive and cleanse us.

10. God wants us to call on Him and to cast our burdens and cares on Him.

11. We know that God will answer with our best interests at heart.

12. (a) Pray with thanksgiving. (b) Give thanks for everything. (Leader: Encourage the ladies to think of specific things God has done for them. God wants us to pray with thanksgiving, no matter what the circumstances may be.)

13. We should end our prayers in Jesus' name, or for His sake.

14. (Leader: For your personal preparation, read the context of each of the passages. Be prepared to describe each situation before you ask the ladies to tell how the characters prayed.) (a) Samson asked God to help him avenge his enemies one last time. (b) Jonah prayed for deliverance from the fish's belly. (c) Peter cried out to the Lord as he sank into the water. (d) The dying thief asked Jesus for salvation.

15. We are in a battle against spiritual, not physical, forces.

LESSON 6

1. Parents should teach their children diligently and consistently in the home, taking advantage of opportunities throughout the day. Parents should bring up their children in the ways of God, according to His Word.

2. Children learn best by example, by watching their parents and other significant adults in their lives pray.

3. Possible answers include observing an adult having his or her own personal devotions (reading God's Word and praying); kneeling with a child to pray at bedtime; hearing adults pray in church; hearing an adult pray on the phone with someone in need; hearing an adult pray consistently at mealtimes; praying with children before they leave for school; hearing an adult say, "Let's pray about that," and then doing so.

4. (a) We teach them by what they see and by removing wicked things from their sight. (b) They learn through watching the godly example of others. (c) We teach them by telling them what God has done for us, our families, our nation, others they know, and so forth.

5. Videos that present the lives of men and women of prayer, such as Daniel or Joseph; full-length biographies for older children; talking books; coloring books for younger children; cassette tapes and CDs; children's Christian Web sites.

6. (a) God is always with us; He will never leave us. (b) God knows all

our troubles. (c) God always sees us. Verses like these teach children that God is everywhere and will hear their prayers anytime, not only at meals and bedtime.

7. Government is ordained by God. We should respect the position that government officials hold, and we should pray for them.

8. We can teach children to ask God for strength from Him. He will help them through their troubles and fears.

9. Our children belong to God, and we must release them back into His will and care.

10. The most important thing for which to pray is our children's salvation.

11. Answers will vary. Here are some possible verses: Psalm 25:4, 5; Psalm 27:14; Psalm 37:3, 4; Psalm 56:11; Psalm 71:1; Proverbs 4:14, 23; Proverbs 15:1.

12. (a) Continue to pray in love. (b) Keep praying because God is faithful to His promise to hear us. (c) Be steadfast; our labor of love and prayers are not in vain in the Lord.

13. Our weapons are not carnal; they are spiritual. They are mighty through God and are able to pull down Satan's stronghold.

14. If two are agreed, God will answer.

15. That the entire household would serve the Lord.

16. God says that if we call on Him, He will answer and show us great and mighty things.

17. A wife is to submit to her husband. That does not mean that she is to be a doormat or a slave, but rather a partner in the marriage. The husband is given the responsibility to make the ultimate decision for the good of the family if he and his wife disagree.

18. Answers will vary, but here are six possible responses: protection from temptation; finances; wisdom at his job and with the children; a humble spirit; strength to live a godly life; health.

19. (a) Pray for unity in the marriage. (b) Pray that the husband develops God's love for his family. (c) Pray that the husband will lead the family with wisdom from God.

LESSON 7

1. Various answers. (Leader: As the ladies respond, list on a chalkboard or overhead transparency the positions of leadership in your church. In a second column list the names of the people who fill those posts. Encourage

the ladies to write the list on paper and take it home, adding it to their prayer journals.)

2. We should uplift our leaders in prayer, especially those who share the Word of God with us.

3. (a) He would ask for prayer for protection from evil forces and that his preaching would have free course and be glorified. (b) That he would live honestly and uprightly before his people.

4. Various answers. (Leader: Again list the needs on the chalkboard or overhead transparency. Emphasize spiritual needs, such as salvation, Christian growth, and unity in the church, as being very important. Then list other needs: physical, medical, financial, children's needs, the elderly, etc. The ladies might want to offer their own prayer needs. Encourage them to copy the list on paper and add it to their journals at home. In their journals, they may want to link specific names to specific needs.)

5. God is pleased with the prayers of the righteous, and His ears are open to them. He is willing and eager to answer.

6. Various answers. (Leader: Emphasize that missionaries are "people," just like everyone else. They have the same needs, heartaches, disappointments, and joys that others have. But the attacks from Satan can be much greater because of the work they endeavor to do. They are worthy of our diligent prayer and concern.)

7. Revival will come only as we believers humble ourselves, confess our sins and are cleansed, and have unity with one another. (Leader: Point out that 2 Chronicles 7:14 is used frequently in this study guide because it is such a powerful, comprehensive verse that challenges us to have humility and clean hearts as we pray before the Lord.)

8. The six blessings are that we will rejoice; He will bestow mercy on us; He will grant salvation to the lost; He will speak peace to those who believe; we will not turn back into "folly" (sin); and God's glory will dwell in our land. (The last blessing listed would apply directly to Israel.)

9. "Make me clean. Renew my spirit, making it right."

10. "Revive us, Lord, and work in our hearts!" Each person should pray for the Lord to work in her own heart; then revival will occur individually and corporately.

11. We should be glad and rejoice that we have the privilege to gather together and worship the Lord.

12. (a) Any iniquity, or sin, separates us from the Father. (b) Division

among us Christians hinders our prayers.

13. (a) The disciples met for prayer after Jesus left them when He ascended back to Heaven. (b) New believers were steadfast, or unfaltering, about meeting to be taught, to fellowship, to eat, and to pray. (c) The disciples came up with a plan that would allow them to give their time wholly to studying and preaching God's Word and to praying.

LESSON 8

1. The wickedness of the human heart, our sinful nature, causes us to speak evil.

2. (a) Pride. (b) A revengeful spirit. (c) A judgmental spirit. (d) An unforgiving spirit. (e) Self-glory, jealousy, and envy. (f) Bitterness. (g) Lack of love.

3. "Busybodies" who walk "disorderly."

4. (a) They can cause bad feelings between best friends and can cause division among believers. (b) We are to avoid them.

5. Yes. Every word is important to God, even our idle (ineffective, useless, vain) words because we will give account for our words.

6. He equates a busybody with a murderer, a thief, or an evildoer.

7. (a) We should not be as the wicked, having deceitful tongues, full of evil. (b) We should bridle our mouths and speak no wicked words.

8. (a) Our whole bodies. (b) Bits in horses' mouths, helms in ships driven by fierce winds, a fire, a world of iniquity, unruly evil, and deadly poison. (c) A mouth speaking blessing and cursing, a fountain spouting sweet and bitter at the same time, a fig tree bearing olive berries, a vine bearing figs, and a fountain giving both salt *and* fresh water. (d) A wise person has knowledge, a good "conversation" (lifestyle), and works filled with meekness and wisdom. (e) Confusion and every evil work. (f) A person who has godly wisdom is pure, peaceable, gentle, easy to be entreated (not judgmental), full of mercy, full of good "fruits" (works), without partiality (favoritism), without hypocrisy, filled with righteousness, and a maker of peace.

9. We don't need to know all the facts. When we don't know what to pray, the Spirit helps us.

10. (a)

Discernment	Judgment
Proverbs 25:2	Proverbs 14:15; 18:13
A discerning person does research to find out all the facts. She doesn't	A judgmental person believes everything, lacks prudence (tact, careful-

accept as true everything she reads or hears.	ness, discretion), and responds before hearing the entire matter.
Galatians 6:1 A discerning Christian restores a fallen Christian, knowing that she herself is subject to temptation, rather than feeling superior to the fallen one.	Matthew 7:1-5 A judgmental person condemns others, sees their faults, but fails to discern her own faults (or chooses to ignore them).

(b) The Spirit-led Christian will be understanding, will not respond immediately before hearing all of a matter, and will humbly help to restore a fallen sister in Christ. The Spirit-led Christian will *not* be willing to believe every report, form opinions about matters before hearing all the facts, and judge someone else for the same or greater sin that she has in her own life.

11. (a) Love them. (b) Do not repay them with evil, but be honest. (c) Be kind, tenderhearted, and forgiving.

12. A true friend will love with a pure love from God, never trying to do evil, but will be kind, tenderhearted, and forgiving.

13. A true friend will not seek to gossip about you nor sit in those circles where gossip is done. She will thank God for your friendship. She will pray that you will grow in love, knowledge, and judgment. She will pray that you will be worthy of God's calling in your life and that God can work through your faith and His power. She will pray that your life will glorify Christ.

14. You could say, "Let's pray for that person right now" or "Let's talk to her now [call her now] and see if that's true" or "Let's go together to the pastor and discuss how we can help the situation" or "I'd rather not hear all those details. I'll just remember to pray for that need."

15. (Leader: Have the ladies read/say the verse together a few times. Make certain they understand terms such as "corrupt communication," "edifying," and "grace.")

LESSON 9

1. God created everything in the universe. Everything in the universe declares God, the Creator.

2. God is the unexcelled, powerful, majestic, and magnificent triune God. (Leader: Each verse mentions attributes of God. The last one cites that God is triune: the Father, the Son, and the Holy Spirit.)

3. (a) God created the man and woman and told them to eat from any tree but the tree of the knowledge of good and evil. (b) The Israelites had a choice: whom to serve. (c) Today is the day of salvation. Summary: God created mankind with a soul and the free will to make choices. (Leader: Discuss the choices mentioned in the verses. In the Garden of Eden, mankind was given the choice to obey or to disobey. The Israelites were given the choice to put away false gods and serve the Lord only or to follow after false gods. People are given the choice to accept God's plan of salvation or to reject it.)

4. (a) God is great, and there is no one else like Him. (b) What God does will last forever and cannot be altered by anyone. (c) God never tires. No one could or will ever figure Him out. (d) God's ways and thoughts are infinitely higher than our ways and our thoughts. Summary: God and His ways are far beyond human understanding.

5. (a) God was God before He created everything. He will eternally remain God. (b) God's power is great; His understanding has no end. (c) God is the only God. He is eternal, immortal, invisible, and wise. Summary: God is infinite.

6. All people will die. They (we) are not immortal.

7. God made people in His likeness, made them male and female, and gave them dominion "over all the earth."

8. (a) The heavens. (b) The invisible things. The heavens and the earth and even the marvels of the microscopic world display God's handiwork so that mankind is without excuse.

9. No. We are not equal with God. He made us out of the dust; gave us flesh, bone, and skin; and made us a little lower than the angels.

10. He made us to worship Him and to bring Him glory and pleasure.

11. (a) The church members at Corinth. They had the choice to examine themselves to see if they were true believers in Jesus Christ. (b) The Christians at Thessalonica. They had the choice to test all things in their lives to learn if they were "good" or "bad." Then they had the choice to hold onto what is good or to let it go. (Leader: Point out that as church members and believers, we have the same choices as the people to whom Paul wrote in Corinth and Thessalonica. Ask: Are you a true believer in Jesus Christ? If you are, are you holding fast [securely] to that which is good?)

12. God does His will, and mankind has absolutely no control over any part of it.

13. (a) God's wisdom and knowledge are a mystery that we cannot

understand fully. (b) On this side of Heaven we see God as though we are looking at Him through translucent glass, unable to see everything clearly. But one day in Glory we shall see Him face-to-face, and we'll have greater understanding.

14. (a) God never changes. (b) For those who love God, all things work together for good. (Leader: Discuss things we consider "bad" [financial loss, death of loved one, etc.] and how God is using all for our ultimate good.) (c) We are to get to know God better. As we are conformed to His image, or become more like Him, He gives us power. (d) Jesus Christ should be glorified in our lives and we in Him as we receive His grace to live for God. (e) We will see Jesus more clearly as we pray and draw closer to Him. We will realize more fully that He lowered Himself to become one of us and to die for our sins. He, too, deserves the glory and honor due the Father, Who, because of His grace, planned for Christ to die for us. (f) Nothing or no one is hidden from our God. He knows about all things. (g) Without faith it is impossible to please God. (Leader: Point out that it is God's will for all of these Scriptural truths, along with many others not discussed, to become life-changing realities in the Christian's life.)

15. (a) We will develop a reverential fear of God, and we will want to keep His commandments. (b) As we seek to know His will for our lives, we will be conformed to His image. (c) We will realize that it is only reasonable that we give our bodies for service to the One Who saved us from an eternity in Hell. We should be living sacrifices, holy and acceptable to God. This is the perfect will of God for each one of us. (d) As we pray, we will begin to develop the desires of God, because we will learn more about "the mind of Christ"; i.e., what He wants each of us to do with our lives to please Him.

LESSON 10

1. (a) Harboring unconfessed sin in our lives. (b) The shedding of blood—possibly murder, abortion, etc.—and "doing evil." (c) Selfishness. We ask for things that feed our own selfish desires and lusts.

2. (a) God does not hear the prayer of the wicked. (b) Our sins separate us from God; He will not hear us. (c) John 9:31—God does not hear sinners.

3. (a) Although Cornelius was an unsaved man, God granted his request to have Simon Peter (v. 32) come to preach to a group of people. Cornelius was saved because of the answered prayer. God chooses to answer the prayer of the lost if the ultimate end brings the soul to a saving knowledge

of Christ. (b) The Lord hears a cry for His salvation.

4.

Reference/Character	How the Character Felt	Unconfessed Sin?
1 Kings 19:1-4—Elijah	He felt so forsaken that he asked God to let him die.	Yes, lack of faith. After defeating the prophets of Baal (1 Kings 18:18-40), Elijah lost his confidence in Jehovah God and ran from Jezebel.
Lamentations 3:44, 54, 55—Jeremiah, the writer	He felt as though the people's "cloud" of sin was blocking any prayer from reaching Heaven; as though he were drowning, cut off from God and forsaken; and in the depths of despair.	No. He had been imprisoned because he took a stand for God. His feeling of being forsaken was due to the Israelites' sins, not his.
Jonah 2:5—Jonah	He felt that the waters that threatened to drown his body were also drowning his soul.	Yes, disobedience. Jonah had sinned by running away from God's leading in his life to go to Nineveh and preach.
2 Corinthians 12:7, 8—Paul	He felt frustrated, perhaps—because he had prayed three times for a physical infirmity to be removed, but God answered no.	No. Paul had no sin in his life that was keeping his prayer from being heard. Although he had prayed three times for the removal of the "thorn in the flesh," he was convinced God answered his prayer with a no answer to teach him that God's grace is sufficient (v. 9).

5. God gives His best to those who have patience and wait for His perfect will in their lives.

6. (a) Verse 27 reminds us that the new generation of Israelites agreed to hear and do the words of the Lord. Thus He would then hear their voices when they cried out to Him. (b) God hears our voices and cries. He knows when we are in distress and need Him. (c) The Lord heard the cry of righteous David and delivered him. He will do the same for us. (d) God heard and answered the prayers of men in the Old Testament who called upon His name.

7. (a) Omnipotence—God never tires and never sleeps. He watches and cares for us all the time. (b) Omnipresence—God the Holy Spirit is with us everywhere we go. Omniscience—The thoughts God has for us are more than the sand of the sea. We are constantly in His watch care. (c) Love—God draws us with His great, eternal love. (d) Mercy and faithfulness—We should have hope because God's mercies give us life. His compassions never fail and are new every morning. His faithfulness is great.

8. (a) To speak from the heart, not with meaningless recitations. (b) Praying in Jesus' name, that is, praying through Him for access to the Father and praying in His will. (c) Keeping the Lord's commandments and seeking to please Him.

9. (a) He states outright that if we ask, we will receive. (b) Jesus said that when we pray for His will, it will be accomplished. (c) John stated that we "know" our petitions are answered.

10. We should remind ourselves that God's grace is sufficient to see us through any trial and any prayer request that we feel He has not answered. In our weakness we become strong in Him.

11. We should request (a) the kingdom of God (that is, God's rule in our lives) and His righteousness, (b) that the Holy Spirit guide our lives, and (c) wisdom.

12. He delights in giving us answers to prayer because we are His children.

13. (a) Joshua—the sun and moon stood still as Joshua had asked. (b) Hannah—God gave her the son she requested. (c) Solomon—God gave Solomon wisdom, more than any king before or since. God also granted him untold wealth and honor (v. 13). In addition, God promised Solomon long life if he would keep God's statutes and commandments (v. 14). (d) Elijah—He called on Jehovah God to reveal His power and called for fire to consume his soaking wet altar. God did so without hesitation.

14. (a) Jesus healed the leper. (b) Jesus saved the disciples from perishing in their boat during a bad storm. (c) Jesus healed Bartimaeus. (d) God healed the nobleman's son who was dying. (e) Peter prayed for the power to raise a woman from the dead. It was done. (f) The Christians in Jerusalem prayed for Peter in prison. God sent an angel to release him.

15. (a) Although God had already directed Gideon to lead the Israelites against the enemy, Gideon prayed twice for two miracles from God to confirm his calling. God answered, showing Gideon without question that

he was the one God wanted to use. (b) Nehemiah wanted to see the walls of Jerusalem rebuilt. So he asked God to cause the king to give him permission to return to Jerusalem to rebuild the walls himself. Nehemiah was granted permission to do the task. (c) After Jesus' ascension, the Christians in Jerusalem asked God for power to preach and heal the sick in Jesus' name. God granted their request, making them missionaries who spread the gospel throughout the known world. (d) Paul prayed day and night for Timothy, but he also took the time and effort to mentor Timothy and to encourage him.

16. (Leader: Ask the ladies if they want to share their thoughts about these prayers and Bible passages. Have any of them prayed the prayer, claimed the verse, and "put feet" to their request? How did they do it? What was the result?)